WHY IS IT TAKING ME SO LONG TO BE BETTER?

WHY IS IT TAKING ME SO LONG TO BE BETTER?

DAVID EDWARDS

Building the New Generation of Believers

COOK COMMUNICATIONS MINISTRIES
Colorado Springs, Colorado • Paris, Ontario
KINGSWAY COMMUNICATIONS LTD
Eastbourne, England

NexGen® is an imprint of
Cook Communications Ministries, Colorado Springs, CO 80918
Cook Communications, Paris, Ontario
Kingsway Communications, Eastbourne, England

WHY IS IT TAKING ME SO LONG TO BE BETTER?
© 2004 by David Edwards

First Printing, 2004
Printed in the United States of America
1 2 3 4 5 6 7 8 9 10 Printing/Year 08 07 06 05 04

Unless otherwise noted, Scripture quotations are taken from the NEW
AMERICAN STANDARD BIBLE®, Copyright © 1960, 1962, 1963,
1968, 1971, 1972, 1973, 1975, 1977, 1995 by The Lockman
Foundation. Used by permission.

Cataloging-in-Publication Data on file with the Library of Congress

ISBN 0781441404

*To **Flipopoly:** You've lived life with a godly passion and confidence that has enabled me to see the answers to life that never fail. I'm forever grateful.*

*To **Richard and Marilyn:** The heart holds the most important commitments in life. The friendship we share rises to the top of my heart. Thanks for being my committed friends and for helping me know how to answer the questions for life.*

CONTENTS

ACKNOWLEDGMENTS

I couldn't have written this book alone. Here are some of the people who helped make it happen.

Trey Bowden: Well, I guess I won't miss a chance to say thank you for your friendship and the great partnership in ministry. Most of all, for watering the rocks in my head.

Janet Lee: You had the vision and insight to set this project in motion. You believed in the value of these books and the impact they will have on thousands of people seeking answers to the questions of life.

Trevor Bron: You took my loaves and fishes and helped multiply them beyond my wildest dreams. A single book becomes a series. Thanks for blessing my life.

Bobby McGraw: I'm still struggling to find your breaking point. Full-time student, pastor—and you still had the time and energy to transcribe this entire project. Wouldn't have happened without you. Your work has been stellar.

Jim Lynch Everybody! You're my friend, my personal doctor who kept me alive—and you drove the comedy engine so well. Better peace through science. Thanks to Eric and Jim Hawkins, for the extra comedy fuel; it helped keep the engine going.

Gary Wilde: Thank you for your surgical editing skills. You preserved the integrity of the manuscripts, communicating the truths that needed to be told, while laughing at my jokes.

Shawn Mathenia: You finally got your very own line in one of my books. *This is it.* Thank you for your friendship and for looking out for me.

Ken Baugh and Frontline: Thank you for your continued passion that shows up in your ongoing work to reach a new generation. You guys are my home away from no home.

The Sound Tracks: Train, Dave Matthews Band, Dave Koz, The Rippingtons, and Journey. Thanks for the inspiration.

The Questions for Life Series

I had just finished speaking at the White House and was eating lunch at Union Station with a young political consultant. We were halfway through our meal when I asked her, "What's life like for a postmodern inside the Beltway? You know, what kinds of questions do they ask?"

"They ask questions about the suffering and wrong in the world," she said, "about the church, and about who Jesus really is. You know, the questions that never fade."

Questions that never fade

Her label for those questions rose up inside of me, and this series of books flowed from that conversation. Postmoderns come wired with the need to answer the questions you'll find in these pages.

Most postmoderns have rejected the pat answers offered by today's spiritual leaders because they have found them to be inadequate for the daily life they face. They have seen others who accepted the ready-made answers but who still struggle making life work. They have no desire to repeat such mistakes. Instead, they challenge the real-life validity of the quick and easy answers.

The questions remain, but some of the questioners let their need for adequate answers diminish into the background. They give way to an apathy that says, "I've got more important things to do in my life than pursuing life's big questions." For others, finding resolution remains a priority. Yet even for them, life can become a never-ending "round-robin" of seeking solutions through new experiences.

Regardless of where you are at the moment, realize that the questions for life never truly fade away. They keep coming back, especially amidst your most trying times. They will keep knocking at your heart's door until you turn and acknowledge their crucial role in finding the life of your dreams. Until you take hold of real explanations, you'll remain constantly searching for the answers that never fail.

Answers that never fail

Spoken or unspoken, identified or unidentified, real answers are priceless. Until we find them, we're haunted by a lack of resolution in life. This unsettled life suffers constant turmoil and never-ending trouble. We look for direction that seems nonexistent, and this makes many of our decisions hard to live with. What price would we pay for a better way?

It's possible to spend a lifetime searching and never finding. Therefore, some would say that the reward comes not in the security of reaching the goal, but in the striving to obtain it. To these people I say: Why waste your life *looking* when you could be *living?*

The Creator of the universe holds the indelible answers we seek. They are not hidden, but they have often been obscured. They are veiled by some who place a higher value on *knowing* the answers than upon allowing the answers to change their lives. We need to push through and ask: What is the actual value of discovering answers that never fail? We'll find the value shining through in *what the answers produce in our lives*. When we discover these answers, our lives change in four supernatural ways. Finding them ...

Builds our outlook It's impossible to live a satisfying life without faith, meaning, and purpose. That's why each of us will place our faith in something or someone that is our primary value. We believe this person or thing will bring meaning and purpose to our life.

Without purpose, we'd have no reason to exist. So even the most cynical and withdrawn person seeks meaning in life. It may reside in something as mundane as keeping a pet iguana fat and happy. Or it could be that he finds meaning in something as twisted as making records and sleeping with young boys.

But life without an ultimate meaning and purpose becomes fragmented and chaotic. We roam from place to place, relationship to relationship, experience to experience, hoping to find something worth living for that endures. The iguana won't live forever. We also quickly discover that people fail us, that work is never-ending, that merely accumulating sensory experiences leads us down a continually darkening pathway.

There is no sense to life without meaning and purpose. There is no meaning and purpose without faith. And there is no faith until we answer the questions that never fade.

Brings ownership Discovering answers to the questions for life transforms us from merely being alive to actually having a life to live. We've all seen people who seem to just take up space in the world. They live for no apparent purpose. The things they do carry no meaning and make no appreciable impact on the people around them. They are alive, but they do not own a life.

> 66 Ownership of life begins when our head and our heart come together at a long-sought crossroads: where the questions that never fade meet the answers that never fail. 99

The questions for life can't be glibly answered, nor should they be made impotent through intellect. They must be answered in our hearts; they must settle down into the very center of our person. Ownership of life begins when our head and our heart come together at a long-sought crossroads: where the questions that never fade meet the answers that never fail.

Breaks us open Every question for life has a spiritual dimension. We may assume that answering the question of world hunger and suffering is only a physical matter, but that would be a wrong assumption. This question first finds its answer in a spiritual dimension, then the physical needs can be addressed in practical action. The same is true for all other questions for life; they each have a spiritual dimension.

The questions for life demand *powerful* answers that remain *present,* regardless of circumstance. The answers that never fade literally open us up to the things of God. That is, they lead us to find and apply his *power* and *presence* to the very heart of our question. These answers don't create despair; they settle disputes. They don't cause confusion; they construct a viable contract between life and us.

Brings an outworking Answering the questions for life develops an internal faith expressed in our observable behaviors. In other words, when we own the answers that never fail, our life takes on a meaning that others see and desire. This outworking of faith is extremely practical. It influences the choices we make, the words we speak, and the attitudes we reflect in daily life.

And this outworking can't help but grow a deep confidence within us. When never-failing solutions calm our internal struggles, we are able to move forward amidst seemingly insurmountable odds. We can work in an environment hostile to the things of Christ—and still live out our faith. We are confident that, although those around us may reject us, we are forever accepted by the One who matters most.

In these books, I have refused to "reheat" the old teachings. Instead of serving leftovers, I've dished up biblical answers that really do apply to the lives we live. These books keep it real, and I've written them with you in mind. I've used generous doses of humor and plenty of anecdotes (most of which actually happened to me).

I've made scant reference to other Christian authors, though, for a reason. In my attempt to make these books fresh, I chose to keep them uncluttered by the thoughts of others. Instead, I try to communicate God's thoughts from the Bible straight to your heart.

You'll notice that the title of each book forms a question. The titles of each chapter also appear as questions. But the content of each chapter *answers* that chapter's question. When read in their entirety, the chapters together answer the big question posed by each book.

You can read these books in any order; they each stand on their own in dealing with a single topic. At the end of each book you'll find questions that I hope will encourage an expanded discussion of the subject matter. Why not bring a group of friends together to talk things through?

Although this book series began over lunch inside the Beltway of Washington, D.C., I am aware that we are all bound together by the questions that never fade. As you read, I hope you will find the answers that never fail.

David Edwards
Summer, 2004

Introduction to
Why Is It Taking Me So Long to Be Better?

It wasn't going to be a long flight, but the timing was critical. I was headed from Oklahoma to a speaking engagement in Kentucky, and a private pilot had volunteered to take me in his small, single-engine plane. We had just enough time for me to arrive with forty minutes to change clothes and get to my speaking destination.

We boarded the plane under a bright sun and almost no wind. We landed in Missouri to refuel and quickly resumed our flight. Thirty minutes later, we flew into a huge storm. My pilot friend said, "We're flying into a storm, but I don't want you to be scared."

"Thanks, but I'm not worried," I said. "Only famous people die in these single-engine planes, and nobody knows who I am."

My friend intently studied the instrument panel, listening to his headset, all the while looking quite in control. I tried to imitate his cool demeanor, but on the inside I was screaming, "AAAHHHHHH!" By this time, I wasn't saying a word, but I was taking in every facet of the experience. The wind tossed us around like a toy, the rain made it impossible to see out of the windshield, and my pilot friend ... pulled out a map.

This is no time to be reading! I thought. Visibility was zero, so he flew completely by instrument. In my own headset, I listened to the tower: "The wind is blowing you off course, correct course to ..." I tried to remain calm, but it wasn't easy.

We were getting lower and lower, but I still couldn't see a thing. I had to trust the pilot, and he had to trust his instruments and the tower to tell him what to do. The wind never let up, the rain never diminished, and the lightning still snapped out at our airborne cocoon. I wasn't sure how much more of this mid-air drama I could take, when suddenly the clouds parted. I saw the runway's blue lights just three hundred feet below.

I'll never forget those clouds parting just before we landed. That image conveys exactly what God has been doing since he placed humans on the earth. The Bible says humans were born into this world with a cloud over their hearts, a cloud covering their vision, and they are unable to see the truth. But God has made a way for us to connect with his presence, and to do it safely. He has laid out a path to life, a place where you and I can connect with Christ and experience soul-deep change.

The apostle Peter begins to answer our questions and concerns about how the life of Christ makes change possible. His life brings about change in three ways:

It releases possibility

As to this salvation.

—1 Peter 1:10

The life of Christ, his coming into our world, releases possibility. It was not an accident, nor was it unexpected. In fact, many who studied and understood the Scripture anticipated his coming and the possibilities for change that he would bring to humanity.

The beginning of the life of Christ predates the moment he was born in the manger. In the ultimate sense, of course, it never began, because Christ is eternal and never created. But the promise of *the life of Christ for us* originated all the way back in the Garden of Eden when God said to Adam and Eve, "I am going to bring my offspring into this world, and my offspring will crush the offspring of the serpent" (see Genesis 3:15). This was the first prediction that Christ would come and break into this world in order to bring the possibility of change.

Christ was expected; therefore, we know for sure that we can change. That is, God created the world and set everything into motion so he could work in our lives. When we touch the life of Christ, it is because God set the life of Christ into motion. He prophesied his Son's coming through the prophets of the Old Testament. The life of Christ, which we are able to experience, makes practical change possible.

It results in personhood

Obtaining as the outcome of your faith the salvation of your souls.

—1 Peter 1:9

The practical outcome of the life of Christ is that he comes to live within us. He begins to change us from the inside out, making us authentic and bringing us into line with the way we were created to be. The life of Christ is not theoretical; it is intensely practical.

> **God doesn't pick out people whom he likes in order to give them special passes into his kingdom.**

It is not creepy or mysterious, and it's not otherworldly. Nor does it happen independent from our unique personalities and circumstances. God meets us, as we are, where we are, and with what we have.

God doesn't pick out people whom he likes in order to give them special passes into his kingdom. It's not an exclusive club. God understands us just the way we are; he gets us. God created each one of us, and he knows what is going on inside of us. He takes our screwed-up or otherwise twisted lives and, wherever we are, uses our choices and circumstances to help us connect to his life. He meets us at the most practical levels of life. It is his life in us that brings authenticity to our personhood.

It is rich in productivity

Though you have not seen Him, you love Him.

—1 Peter 1:8

Something is rising up inside of us, because the life of Christ is productive. It is impossible to meet Christ and not be changed. When we collide with the life of Christ, something begins to happen inside of us. Though we don't see him, we believe in him.

Our generation distrusts authority and avoids structure, so we think, "If anything is going to happen, I have to do it myself." As a result, we attempt to live under our own authority, and we get into all kinds of trouble. Our life blows up and shatters into a thousand pieces.

Biblical Christianity teaches that if transformational change is going to happen in us, Christ will be the cause. His life makes us who we are becoming: Christlike. He changes us from the inside out.

> *Beloved, now we are children of God, and it has not appeared as yet what we shall be. We know that when He appears, we will be like Him, because we will see Him just as He is.*
>
> *—1 John 3:2*

Christ has come into the world and brought with him new life that is exciting, daring, subversive, and most of all, freeing. It opens up for us another way to live. It gives our success, our purpose, and our suffering the meaning we are

> 66 Authoritative answers abound but are mostly filled with conjecture, speculation, and confusion. The average believer is left more disillusioned than satisfied. 99

searching for. The only platform for change that people like us have is established inside the life of Christ. It can only be discovered there.

Those are the themes we'll be exploring together in the chapters to come. I've organized these chapters into three major sections to help you see the Christian life and understand the acceptable growth rate:

Chapter 1: The Encouragement to the Christian Life.
Chapters 2 and 3: The Energy of the Christian Life.
Chapters 4 through 7: The Experience of the Christian Life.

I hope this book helps many beleivers understand why the Christian life seems not to be working for them. This subject is perhaps the most misunderstood of all the practical theology we can learn. Authoritative answers abound but are mostly filled with conjecture, speculation, and confusion. The average believer is left more disillusioned than satisfied.

I see spiritual growth as the natural product of a personal relationship with Jesus Christ. My hope is that, as you read, you'll keep an open mind and an open heart. You may find some unique ideas here, some things you've never heard before at church. Nothing is meant to shock you, though—but to invite you into a deeper search of the Scriptures and a more focused pursuit of an intimate relationship with Christ. I've also thrown in lots of humor because, after all, laughing is a part of the good life Christ has come to give us. Enjoy!

IS THERE ANY HOPE FOR ME?

C hurches hold thousands of revival services across the United States each year. These services always culminate with altar-invitations that follow essentially the same order, regardless of location. The speaker tells a sad story about some poor guy getting hit by a tractor and dragged into eternity, separated from Christ forever. Regardless of the obvious plot flaw that even *I* could outrun a tractor, the story still frightens people down the aisle. Then it's time for the sad song to be played on the organ—over and over again— backed up by a humming choir. Finally, the speaker begins to close the deal.

When I've been in these situations, some of the things I've heard speakers say don't make much sense to me. But they all seem to say the same things ...

"If you're here tonight ..." I always want to raise my hand and ask him where he thought we'd been for the past forty-five minutes.

"Every head bowed, and every eye closed; no one is looking

around ..." And there I am, standing there with my head up and my eyes open, looking around the room trying to make eye contact with someone else who shared my thoughts.

"*I won't embarrass you ...*" But then he asks people to raise their hands before calling them out, "Yes sir, I see you standing back there, the bald one by the lady with the blue hair. Yes, *you!*"

"*Everyone, stand to your feet ...*" What other options do we have? What else do you stand up on?

"*Now turn over in your hymnal ...*" Have you ever actually tried that? Even a contortionist would need a chiropractor for a solid year.

This is what most of us know of the soul-saving invitation. But when we look back at what Jesus did, and the way he extended the invitation, don't we see a much different picture? Most likely he gave hundreds of invitations in his lifetime, but they were very different from what we know. Throughout his earthly ministry, Jesus invited many people to "Follow me." They either decided to do it, or they decided not to do it.

That was pretty much it. There was no music, and there was no choir. There weren't even any sad stories about lost puppies. Jesus' invitations flowed naturally from something he was speaking about—or they were offered within the context of a relationship. He would simply say, "Follow me."

In his revolutionary way, Jesus broke into human history and established such a dynamic around his invitation that we struggle just to comprehend the power behind it. It wasn't just a walk down an aisle to sign a card and check a box. For Jesus, the invitation was about the whole of one's life. The invitation knew no boundaries, there were no fences, and there were no prejudices. The invitation was always going out from him to everyone around him.

This generation seems discouraged about responding to Christ. We tend to think that Christianity was created only for the people who can do it— the religious insiders, people who grew up in church and know something about the Bible. There have been moments in my own life when I doubted whether I could sign on and keep the commitment. I project myself back into New Testament days, following along in a crowd behind Jesus. I imagine him turning around and saying, "You ... follow me." As I push my way to the front, he says, "No, not *you*. The guy behind you." Even in this scenario, Jesus only calls the ones who can make the grade. Everyone else gets left outside.

> We tend to think that Christianity was created only for the people who can do it—the religious insiders, people who grew up in church and know something about the Bible.

A lot of people think about following Christ and wonder, *Is there any hope for me?* When we understand what the invitation really means, we find that regardless of our background, age or stage, what we've done or what's been done to us, the invitation is for us.

Our journey into the discovery of spiritual growth begins with the invitation. I hope to show, based on a story in Matthew 9, that Jesus really turns the religious world upside down by extending his hand to the most unlikely person. So consider these five statements about the invitation to follow Christ:

The invitation extends to renegades

"As Jesus went on from there, He saw a man called Matthew, sitting in the tax collector's booth; and He said to him, 'Follow Me!' And got up and followed Him" (Matt. 9:9).

Matthew was a tax collector, and I have heard people say, "This guy was hated because he took money from people." That's not the only reason people hated tax collectors, though. A whole chain of tax collectors flourished in Matthew's day. Some men oversaw entire regions, collecting large amounts of taxes. Some were managers who watched over the managers. Then came the small-time operators who sat in booths and imposed random taxes on people as they walked by.

> " When we look closely at the earthly ministry of Jesus, we find him going to people standing on the sidelines of society. "

28

Rome demanded certain quotas, but once the collectors had collected their quotas, anything over and above that figure was theirs to keep. Everyone hated these guys because they were allowed to invent taxes on the spot—and the law backed them. But this is not why Matthew was hated. He was hated because he was being a bad Jew.

Matthew was a Jew doing a Gentile's job. In Jewish eyes, he was a sell-out, one Jew stealing from another Jew. As a result, Matthew and his publican tax-collector friends were banned from the synagogue. This guy was an extreme outsider, not just somebody unacquainted with Jesus.

Matthew and all of his friends kept to themselves and had their own little circle of friends. But then Jesus came along, the Son of God, and turned to Matthew, saying: "You ... follow me." Jesus was known by many to be a great rabbi, and his invitation to this stranger—an outsider, a fugitive, an outlaw—was quite radical. Though banned by the religious system, Matthew receives an invitation.

The invitation comes to any of us who are outlaws and renegades. I'm not referring to a certain lifestyle; I'm using these terms to identify any who have kept their hearts at a distance from God. Good people from the suburbs can be such heart-renegades. Or they may have grown up in less than perfect neighborhoods; they, too, might keep their hearts far from God. But in one way or another, we're all renegades, all outlaws. Jesus turns to all of us and says, "Follow me."

When we look closely at the earthly ministry of Jesus, we

find him going to people standing on the sidelines of society. He went to a Samaritan woman while she was seeking fulfillment in numerous affairs. He said to her, "I know what will make your life work." He extended the invitation.

Zaccheus was another tax collector hated by his fellow Jews. One day Jesus came through town and saw this small man up in a tree and said, "I want you to come down because I'm going to go home and have dinner with you." Jesus always reached out to renegades. He always reached out to people who didn't fit in, who couldn't seem to make life work.

A woman was caught in adultery and thrown down at Jesus' feet. The religious leaders surrounded her, holding rocks, ready to stone her. But Jesus said, "Whoever hasn't committed sin can throw the first stone." One by one, they all dropped their rocks and backed away. Jesus told her, "Your past is of no consequence anymore; go and sin no more."

Next to Jesus' cross hung a thief, a man with no hope for reprieve. His life was over—separated from his family, separated from his government, soon to be separated from his physical life. Jesus turned to this man and said, "Today you will be with me in paradise."

Recently I went out to eat with a group of friends. We sat down, and I looked around the table. *Here are people from such different backgrounds,* I thought. Some came from stable, deeply religious homes; others grew up in the chaos of soap-opera-like family dramas.

Around that table, our lives intersected, because there had

been a moment of invitation for each of us. If we had merely gone to high school together, we'd be sitting at different lunch tables.

Now we had a deeper connection. We'd all responded to the invitation.

The invitation encourages relationship

Many tax-collectors and sinners came and were dining with Jesus and His disciples.

—Matthew 9:10

Matthew took Jesus to his house. He called all his tax collector friends and said, "You've got to come meet this guy."

We think going out to dinner is just eating a meal away from home. In Jesus' day, when someone sat across the table and ate with you, it was a an act of friendship and agreement. It was a big deal for a Jewish rabbi to step into the lives of social screw-ups and say, "I'm going to sit down and hang out with you." Jesus was saying to these men, "I'm going to be in covenant with you. I am not just coming to recruit you for my cause; I am coming to have a friendship with you."

> "The bottom line of Christianity is that it invites us to step into the presence of God. The focus of Christianity is not perfection but connection."

The invitation encourages relationship. The bottom line

of Christianity is that it invites us to step into the presence of God. The focus of Christianity is not perfection but connection. There sat all of these renegades, Matthew's friends,

> **66 The invitation to follow Christ always endangers our routine. 99**

around a table eating a meal with Jesus. Nobody had to pretend in that room. Jesus didn't require these men to be anything other than who they were. Jesus stepped into their natural environment and said, "We're going to relate with each other."

The invitation to *follow* him always encourages us to *connect* with him. We don't have to pretend to be religious. We don't have to act like something we're not. We don't have to put on a front and use a lot of God lingo. We only have to come as we are—good or bad, right or wrong, close to him or far away.

By stepping into Matthew's world, Jesus was not condoning the fact that he had ripped people off. Rather, he stepped into their lives and redeemed them, winning them back to himself. In attitude and actions he said, "Through our relationship I am going to redeem you. I'm going to show you a better way to live."

The invitation endangers our routine

The Son of God, along with his disciples, was having dinner with renegades and outlaws around a table. These guests were shunned by society and the religious system of the day.

The entire religious system was built around the role of the rabbi, whose work was inside the synagogue. That was the place where the scrolls would be read, theology could be debated, and the doctrines discussed.

Obviously, Jesus broke ranks with this entire system and instead took his "rabbinical" ministry to the house of a renegade. The rabbis of his day resented Jesus' departure from their established routine. His radical ways pushed against their comfort zones.

The invitation to follow Christ always endangers our routine. It not only endangered Matthew's routine, it challenged his whole life. Matthew decided to follow Jesus, and as a result, he had to quit his job; it was incompatible with his decision. That is the nature of the invitation. It's messy to say yes to Christ. Accepting the invitation creates tension in families and turns friends into enemies.

The cost is different for each of us. But it *will* cost.

The invitation exposes our need for a new ruler

"Go and learn what this means."

—Matthew 9:13

A rabbi would often use these words with students having trouble learning their lessons. It was a disapproving challenge to study harder. Thus Jesus was sending the religious leaders away and letting the renegades know they needed new rulers.

In everyone's life, two types of "rulers" can be found: Pharisees and physicians. Both have their own agenda and both battle for your acceptance of their invitation. We will each choose one of these as the ruler of our lives.

The Pharisee "When the Pharisees saw this" (Matt. 9:11). Today the Pharisees would be known as the Christian "hall monitors." They ran around passing judgment on everyone saying, "No one deserves the love of God. If God is going to be good to you, it'll be because you keep all the rules. If you deviate from the law, you're out!"

The "Christian hall monitor" mentality coerced, condemned, and convicted people. It coerced people by beating them over the head with the law. It condemned them if their lives seemed out of order. It convicted them for living differently. For some of us, this type of religion has been our only exposure to God!

Some of us actually have a little Christian hall monitor inside us. You can tell by watching your reaction the next time something good happens to someone who is broken and undeserving. The hall monitor thinks, *Well that's not fair. Here I am, I've toed the line, I've been a good Christian person my whole life, and this total screw-up has the blessing of God on him?* A little bit of the Christian hall monitor lives in us all. We all feel the need to vindicate our choices and make sure someone else doesn't get a bigger share of the blessing than we do.

The Physician The hall monitors in Jesus' day approached the disciples and asked, "Why is he eating with all of the outcasts?" These self-appointed judges were too cowardly to take Jesus on personally, so they attacked his followers. "When

Jesus heard this, He said, 'It is not those who are healthy who need a physician, but those who are sick'" (Matt. 9:12).

Jesus, the physician, walked into this place and said, "I didn't come to play religious games or to get people to obey a code of law or ethics. I came for the sick and the broken." This is sort of the first New Testament reality show of "Christ Eye for the Lost Guy."

Matthew's friends gathered in the room that day because they longed for something other than a religious system. Jesus didn't come to them because they were tax collectors; that was a non-issue. He came into that room to provide what they longed for: a new ruler.

The only qualification for following Christ is to know that you need him. That's it. You don't have to be perfect, know a bunch of Bible verses, or be able to spout theology. Matthew didn't know theology or doctrine, but he knew he needed Jesus.

> **The only qualification for following Christ is to know that you need him.**

Jesus saw himself as a physician, someone who went to the broken and the bent and said, "I understand *why* you're the way you are." In the middle of all of our choices, God hears our longings to connect with him. In order for Matthew to follow Christ, the one thing he had to do was to let go of everything that could kill him. This was Jesus' diagnosis: "Matthew, if your life is going to work, you are going to have to let go of the things that are sabotaging your life."

Matthew saw Jesus. Jesus heard his longings and extended the invitation, "Follow me." To do that, Matthew had to let go of everything that was killing his heart.

> 66 Don't expect your particular Christian life to be neat and tidy. There will be lot of drama in it. 99

The invitation establishes a new reason for living

Matthew ... rose and followed Him.
—Matthew 9:9

Matthew's whole life changed direction. He was no longer held hostage by his past, no longer defined by what people said about him. At this defining moment, Matthew was still a tax collector, of course. But now, because he responded to the invitation, he was freed from all his past, no longer held captive by all his previous decisions.

With the invitation to follow Christ, we're given a dangerous freedom. We can step away from all the things that are killing us and step into him. It is the freedom *not* to have life defined by our past mistakes, by the opinion of others, or by the labels people slap on us.

He takes all the risk of rejection; he lets us choose how we will respond to him. Christianity doesn't exist in a book; it is birthed out of a decision just like the one Matthew made: "Alright, you got me; I'm going to follow you. I don't know anything about the Bible, but I'm going to follow you. I don't know how to defend my faith, but I'm going to follow you."

Christianity happens in the context of our real life, just as it is. The challenge is to figure out how a Christian life looks in the context of what we are doing. The relationship we have with Christ looks different for all of us because every life has a different context.

Don't expect your particular Christian life to be neat and tidy. There will be a lot of drama in it. After all, no one ever falls into spiritual maturity; they progress into it as the Holy Spirit works within them. Those who have tried to grow on their own terms—and failed—appreciate the truth that God is the one who engineers our growth. But if we become pre-occupied with our ability and worthiness to follow him, we'll begin to wonder: *How could God love someone like me?*

As with all invitations, there is an R.S.V.P. What will yours be? There is no card to sign and no box to check. At this point, it's enough to say, "I will follow him from where I am with all I have, in the fullest understanding possible. I will trust that he's taking me where I need to be."

Chapter Two

How could God love someone like me?

Do certain people get on your nerves? For instance, what about airline flight crews? I travel almost every day and fly almost everywhere I go. Nothing annoys me more than the way the flight personnel talk about the trip we're taking.

When you're about to get on the plane, they don't just say, "We're all going to get on the plane now." No, that would be too easy. Instead, they say, "We are going to pre-board." Isn't that like getting in *before* you get in? (Nor do they tell you to get off the plane when you arrive. No, that would be the time to "de-plane.")

Then they give that little safety lecture before take-off. They tell you how to use a seatbelt ... just in case you haven't been in a car since 1979. They show you how to buckle it and then how to unbuckle it. (I'm glad they do that because I had tried gnawing my way out of a seatbelt once, not knowing there was a release switch on the buckle.)

During the safety lecture they always say, "In case of a water landing ... (a nice way of saying, 'In case this plane becomes a convertible') ... your seat cushion can be used as a flotation device." Let me just say that if I'm being hurled toward the ground at a thousand miles per hour, my seat cushion is going to be used as a toilet. Someone else can float on it after I'm done with it.

> **" As irritating as people can be, God still loves them. All of them. Even me. "**

I just want them to say what they mean without dressing it up!

Another group that gets on my nerves are those public nail-clipper people. A lady next to me on the plane was clipping her nails—and one big chunk flew into my soda. I could barely restrain myself from turning her in for smuggling a contraband "weapon" onto the plane.

And how about those guys with twenty-eight inch bass-only speaker systems inside their Geo Metros? They pull up next to you at a stoplight and you think you've come under mortar attack by an army of crazed reggae space invaders. You look over to see who, exactly, is crushing the last precious gasps of air out of your lungs—and there's no driver! Wait ... he's just got his seat laid back; his head is one of the passengers.

Anyway, I'm sure you've got your own list of nerve-fraying individuals. But as irritating as people can be, God still loves them. All of them. Even me.

Regardless of our past, and regardless of what we do, God loves us. Yet one of the secret questions many people hold in their hearts is, "How God could ever love someone like me?"

How could God love someone like us? Not to oversimplify it, but the short answer is: God made it possible through his Son, Jesus. In Romans 5, Paul teaches about the death of Jesus and how it affects us. What Jesus did on the cross made us acceptable to God. Paul says: "Therefore, having been justified by faith, we have peace with God through our Lord Jesus Christ" (Rom. 5:1).

Therefore is a big New Testament word that we can understand best as a comma. It's a call back, referring to verses 21 and 24 of chapter 4: "Being fully assured that what God had promised, He was able also to perform. ... But for our sake also, to whom it will be credited, as those who believe in Him who raised Jesus our Lord from the dead" (Rom. 4:21, 24). In these verses, Paul is telling us that Christ's righteousness—his perfect life and his perfect, eternal sacrifice—are credited to our account. It's as if his funds are placed in our bank. When God looks at us, he sees the perfect righteousness of Jesus. That's how acceptable we are!

This is what it means to be justified by faith. We aren't lovable because we are good enough or because we look the part. We are lovable because there was a moment when our lives collided with the life and death of Christ. "Therefore, having been justified by faith, we have peace with God through our Lord Jesus Christ" (Rom. 5:1). We trust Jesus as our righteousness, not our own imperfect works.

But let's break this down and really dig into it. What, exactly, does the death of Jesus do to make us lovable and acceptable to God? His death does at least four things.

It rescues us from the strategy of the world

While we were still helpless, at the right time Christ died for the ungodly. ... But God demonstrates His own love toward us, in that while we were yet sinners, Christ died for us.

—Romans 5:6, 8

According to the Bible, outside of Christ we are helpless, powerless, sinful, and cut off from God's presence. In this condition, our only option is to do what the world tells us to do. The core religious belief of the world is: "Doing right will make me better." Therefore, we falsely believe that as long as we try to do better—as long as we try to do some good humanitarian things, as long as we try to improve our lives and clean ourselves up—that by itself will make us better.

> " The core religious belief of the world is: 'Doing right will make me better.' "

So many people believe they can earn their way into God's presence! This is the thinking of our world; this is its strategy for gaining heaven. All we have to do is make sure our list of good works outweighs our list of bad works before we die. I read an article about a football coach who was not a believer. But he always had a chaplain come in to conduct chapel services before the games.

One player asked, "If you don't believe in Christ, why do you have the chaplain come?"

The coach answered, "I want to make sure God is on my side."

That's crazy! How can anyone think this way? I happen to know that God hates sports.

But this is part of the world's strategy. Sometimes when you see a live concert on television, they'll cut to the backstage camera and show the lead singer and band praying together. Imagine it: "God, please bless our concert before we go out and sing, 'I Used to Love Her, but I Had to Kill Her.'"

We have grown up thinking that we can earn our way to God's acceptance. Yet, the very things that gnaw at us are the mistakes we've made trying to do just that. When we do visualize ourselves walking into the presence of God, we can't help but think, "How could God love me after everything I've done?"

The truth is, we can't ever do enough good things to earn our way into God's presence. So he just holds out his hands, palms forward. At the right time, while we were still sinners, Christ died for us and went to the cross redeeming us. We don't become Christians because we believe in our own goodness. We come to Christ, and he gives us the faith to believe in him. He rescues us from the "doing good" strategy of the world.

It releases us from our screw-ups

If while we were enemies we were reconciled to God through the death of His Son, much more, having been reconciled, we shall be saved by His life.

—Romans 5:10

On the cross, Jesus became the sin magnet for the world. He actually "became sin for us" (see 2 Cor. 5:21). He took everything that we would ever do against God, ourselves, and other people as his own. He took on every bad decision, every scar, every stain, and every screw-up.

I realize that some of this is hard to accept. After all, the consequences of our choices are always in front of us. We may think that all of this sounds great. "But you don't know what I did last night, and you don't know what I did last weekend!" we say. "It's hard for me to believe in justification by faith alone ... and not think that somehow God is still disappointed with what I've done."

Well, it is true that Jesus took on all of our scars and stains. Yet the natural consequences we face—lost opportunities, broken relationships, damaged health or finances—these eat away at us and cause us to think, *Maybe God is secretly disappointed with me, and maybe this will work for everybody else but not for me.*

If we lived in Old Testament days, this fear might be legitimate. To deal with their sin in those days, people had to go down to the local tabernacle and seek out a priest. The priest would then go into the Holy of Holies with the blood of a goat, a bull, or a dove and sprinkle it on the mercy seat, making atonement for the sin. In the Old Testament, sins were *covered* (temporarily, until Jesus came). But in the New Testament, our sins are no longer covered; they are *removed*, taken away. Because of Christ, our sins are separated from us, as though they never happened. They are not tucked away in a file, or even shredded; they are dissipated. All is forgotten and forgiven. To those who feel the weight of their past choices, the Bible declares you don't owe anything.

Christ paid your sin-debt for you. It is forgiven, and it is forgotten.

"It is finished."

We are released from our screw-ups. And when we step into the presence of God, he doesn't come to rub our sins in; he already came to rub them out. This is real life. Our confidence in Jesus is *not* based on our emotion. It is based on what the Word declares about our Savior—who he is and what he did.

It removes the separation

Much more then, having now been justified by His blood, we shall be saved from the wrath of God through Him.

—Romans 5:9

Why was God angry? Because God hates sin. Think all the way back to the Garden of Eden, when Adam and Eve played a cosmic game of Red Rover, breaking ranks with God and siding with the enemy. At that moment, they gave up their right to

> "God hates sin. The result is that the God who loves us is, in a sense, our enemy. Here is serious conflict between God and humanity!"

become children of God. They traded that right to accept a bogus offer from Satan. Thus sin entered into the world. And from that point in time, every person born has been tainted with sin, born separated from God.

God hates sin. The result is that the God who loves us is, in a sense, our enemy. Here is serious conflict between God and humanity!

So Jesus broke into the history of the world and died on the cross. With one hand reaching toward heaven and with the other hand reaching toward humanity, he made peace between God and mankind. We can experience the presence of God because Jesus removed the sin-separation: "You lived in this world without hope and without God. But now, in union with Christ Jesus you, who used to be far away, have been brought near by the death of Christ" (Eph. 2:12–13, Good News Translation).

Imagine if you were living in one part of the globe and God was way off on the other side of the globe somewhere. You know he's real, but he is just not real inside of you. That's what separation from God is like. But then we bring him the real condition of our lives. "Okay, I know I can't earn my way in. I know I can't clean myself up enough to get into your presence. All I can do is place my confidence in the fact that Jesus died on the cross for me. I can allow that reality to collide with my life." At that moment all of our sins, scars, and stains are removed. The separation is gone.

It re-creates our spirit

"If while we were enemies we were reconciled to God through the death of His Son, much more, having been reconciled, will we be saved by His life."

—Romans 5:10

While we were separated from God and still his enemies, the death of Jesus made it possible for us to come back to him. Christ's life makes the re-creation of our spirit possible. This reconciling life of Christ is deposited within us. "Not only this, but we exult in God through our Lord Jesus Christ, through whom we have now received the reconciliation" (Rom. 5:11).

When we chose to believe that Christ's death on the cross rescued us from having to earn our way into God's presence, we were saying, "Lord Jesus, I know that you didn't just die for the world but that you died for *me.*" At that moment the resurrected life of God takes up residence in us. We receive eternal life, a particular *quality* of life that never ends. You see, eternal life is more than just a ticket to heaven. It's more than just the passage of time. It's a kind of life—the life of God— given to those who by faith know him as their leader. It's a life *and* a lifestyle. We live it with a re-created spirit.

Some people say, "What if I choose to believe that—and I don't *feel* anything?" Let's think about that for a moment. First, realize that there are different types of faith. For example, there is *modern faith.* People with this type of faith believe in Christ based mainly on what they understand. This faith stands upon logic, theology, and the study of history. Then there is *postmodern faith.* These folks believe in Christ based mostly on what they can feel during worship and study and quiet. They validate whether something is real or not based on how much feeling there is or isn't.

But we are neither modernists nor postmodernists! We are Christ followers. While facts and feelings have their roles to play, the Christian faith is based on who Jesus is and what he did on the cross. Whether you feel it or not, his life, death, and resurrection are still true. And your theology about these things will never encompass the whole, eternal truth. *Understanding* falls short, just as *feeling* does.

Christianity is not about what we are *doing*, either. It is about what has already been done. Jesus, on the cross, removed the separation between us and God.

You may have started reading this book in a "separated from God" condition. The challenge for you is to close the separation, not by trying to be good but by opening your heart to God. Your prayer might sound something like this: "Jesus, I can't do any more than I've already done, good or bad. All I can do is offer you my life. I place my confidence in your cross. There, all my screw-ups died with you."

> **Jesus doesn't say: 'Hey, man, feel me.' He just says, 'Trust me, rest in me.'**

I met a guy last summer who said, "I became a Christian tonight."

"Has that ever happened to you before?" I asked.

"Oh yes," he said. "Tonight is my twelfth time."

He had no real understanding of salvation. It's a "once and for all" proposition (see Heb. 10:10). But this young man thought it was all about how he was feeling. When he *felt* separated from God, then he figured he *was* in fact separated. Not so! Imagine falling asleep on a train. While you sleep, you don't feel like a passenger. But does that mean you're actually home in bed? Jesus doesn't say: "Hey, man, feel me." He just says, "Trust me, rest in me."

Some of us need to quit thinking for awhile. When we weren't even thinking about God—and when it didn't even matter what God thought about us—Jesus still died for us. Some of us need to quit searching for a feeling, realizing that God loves us in a way we've never before experienced.

How could God love us? Because everything that could make us unlovable was settled in the death of Jesus on the cross. All you and I can do is come to him, in whatever state we're in, and say, "God, I can't. But you can."

God never asks us to accomplish the Christian life in our own strength. God is no spectator, existing on some arid plain, watching with anticipation to see how we'll do. He comes to live inside of us and make us new creatures.

He calls us to know him and to know ourselves in a way impossible to those without Christ. He calls us to this place because he knows that it will produce in us the things we can only dream about.

Chapter Three

WHAT WILL KNOWING CHRIST
DO FOR ME?

The underlying theme of every TV commercial is, "Our product will make your life better, quicker, faster, or cheaper!" Whether hawking cars, clothes, or candy bars, that's what the ads are all about. And we've been conditioned to expect these promises.

I recently saw a commercial for an electronic device that attaches to your abdomen, using electric pulses to contract your stomach muscles. Supposedly, you can wear it around the house or office, experiencing the perfect abs workout while you do other things—like eating deep-fried chalupas and creamy milkshakes.

The psychic commercials are another example, offering a faster, quicker, cheaper way to find life's real answers. I called one of those hotlines when it advertised one free question. They want you to ask nebulous questions about the future, but I said: "Help me out here. I'm holding two cans, and the labels fell off both of them. I just want to know if I'm going to be eating soup or dog food for supper tonight. Let me hold the cans up to the phone." *Click.*

Who doesn't want a better, cheaper, faster, and quicker life? I went to a grocery store and noticed that nearly every product follows this type of thinking. I went down one aisle and found dog food that advertises, "New and improved." I stood there wondering, *What difference is this going to make to Rover?* I read further and the packaging said, "Now with more fiber."

More fiber for your dog. Do we really need dogs with increased regularity? Have you ever been walking your dog when it looks up at you in a way that says, "Got nothing; can you help me out here?"

When it comes to the spiritual side of our lives, we tend to carry "ad think" with us: "What's in it for me? What am I going to get out of this?"

In fact, you may be a God-shopper, "just looking," not ready to commit. So you naturally wonder about the potential benefits: *Why would I want to know Christ?* In Philippians, Paul answers this question for us all. This four-chapter letter flows out of his personal experience of living for Christ for thirty years. Paul had an amazing conversion—thrown from his horse, struck blind, and hearing the voice of Christ saying, "Paul, why are you persecuting me?" From that day forward, he was never the same. The crucifixion, the resurrection, and the ascension all transformed his life in that one moment of time.

What will knowing Christ do for me? The answer comes

to us in the three elements of the essential Christian message: the crucifixion, resurrection, and ascension of Christ. Each of these events is a vital ingredient in creating the energy of the growing Christian life.

> ❝ If anyone ever had reason to boast about a saintly résumé, it was Paul. What an impeccable religious pedigree! ❞

The crucifixion brings confidence

If anyone else has a mind to put confidence in the flesh, I far more.

—Philippians 3:4

In the first several verses of Philippians 3, Paul details his background, telling us that he has every right to demand respect and authority. To help us understand how and why his life was so radically changed, he speaks of where he was *before* he met Christ.

[I was] circumcised the eighth day, of the nation of Israel, of the tribe of Benjamin, a Hebrew of Hebrews; as to the Law, a Pharisee; as to zeal, a persecutor of the church; as to the righteousness which is in the Law, found blameless.

—Philippians 3:5–6

If anyone ever had reason to boast about a saintly résumé, it was Paul. What an impeccable religious pedigree! The

Benjamites were the front-line people in battle. Furthermore, as a Pharisee, Paul had to keep over 1,500 commandments, every single day of his life. Paul was saying, "I not only did it, but I never made a mistake."

Paul was confident in his moral track record—and why not? He came from a religiously perfect tribe and a religiously perfect order. Even though he was a persecutor of the church, in the eyes of the religious elite, he was still excellent, because the Pharisees hated Christians. Paul was saying, "Even in my hatred, I was great!" Even as an elitist, Paul did it right.

Could we equate this type of person with people who grew up in church today? Let's say they came from a religious family, maybe even attended a Christian high school, never got into any trouble, and never did anything even remotely shady. They memorized the Scripture, passed all the tests, did everything expected in the church, and maintained perfect attendance. Someone coming out of this environment may think, "Spiritually, I've got it together."

But how does Paul view his background and accomplishments? "Whatever things were gain to me, those things I have counted as loss for the sake of Christ" (Phil. 3:7). In the big picture, my bragging rights don't mean anything at all.

After having met Christ, Paul realized that all of his religious activity wasn't going to get him into the presence of God. It didn't matter how many laws he kept, how perfect he had been, or how pure his lineage was. On the road to Damascus, when he was confronted by the crucified Christ (see Acts 9), he lost confidence in his religious résumé. He suddenly found his confidence in the presence and person of Jesus Christ.

Have you placed your confidence in what you have done, will do, or are capable of doing for God? Or have you, instead, put your confidence in the fact that Jesus died in your place? Regardless of how good we've been, what mistakes we've made, or what humanitarian things we've done, those things are counted as loss beside knowing that Jesus took everything in our life to the cross with him. Therefore, we trust that we "may be found in Him, not having a righteousness of [our] own derived from the Law, but that which is through faith in Christ" (Phil. 3:9).

Our personal performance actually *prevents* us from experiencing the presence of God. Some of us are so wrapped up with the fact that we've been good. Or that we're better than most people we work with. Or that we haven't done the same horrible things our neighbors have done. Paul says all of that is just rubbish; this type of thinking won't get us anywhere.

Most people, when they travel, act differently than when they're at home. At home, you use one towel. But when you travel, you suddenly start using all the towels. When I travel, I use one towel for each foot, one for each ear, and one for each hand. If there are ten towels, then I will use all of them for one shower and leave them all over the room. If I run out of towels, I make up reasons for the hotel to bring me more.

That's the way we think about our life when it comes to our relationship with God. "Don't I have to clean my life up before I come to God? Don't I need to get my life in order, make everything right and tow the line for a while so God will be more impressed and love me more? Maybe before I give my life to Christ, I should clean it up." He comes into our lives with an unlimited supply of towels.

> **He comes into our lives with an unlimited supply of towels.**

Coming to Christ means that he takes all that we are and we receive all that he is. When this exchange happens, our confidence rests no longer in ourselves but in the Christ who died in our place. The crucifixion produces confidence.

The resurrection produces reason

> *That I may know Him, and the power of His resurrection.*
>
> —Philippians 3:10

The resurrection gives us the reason to live. Before coming to Christ, Paul's purpose for living was to obey the law, toe the line, be perfect, kill Christians, and hate people who didn't agree with his cause. But once he met Christ, the resurrection changed his reason for living.

The fact that Jesus is alive gives us reason to live our own lives to the fullest. Our purpose for living is not to make up for our past failures; that was settled on the cross. Our purpose for living is not to prove that we are good enough for God to love; that became a nonissue when Christ died. Our reason for living now becomes *knowing him.* Paul wanted to know Christ, and he wanted to be conformed to his resurrection. In plain English, Paul wanted the life of Christ to be built in him and released through him.

Paul had experienced Easter for himself. When Christ entered into his life, everything Paul had depended on died, and his life was now only to be found in the new, resurrected life of Christ. When Paul met Christ at the cross, everything that was right or wrong about him had died with the death of Christ. At the same time Jesus was resurrected from the dead, Paul's spirit was also resurrected.

But what if we fail, even after accepting this resurrected life? Our failures, too, were taken care of on the cross—even the future ones. Some of us are still trying to pay off the past or make a down payment on the future. Some of us are living in the grave when there is resurrection life available, right now. The crucifixion produces confidence. The resurrection gives us the reason to live.

> " In plain English, Paul wanted the life of Christ to be built in him and released through him. "

The ascension brings ability

Jesus was killed on a cross, placed in a tomb, and three days later came back to life. In the following days, he appeared to more than five hundred men and women. People talked with him, touched him, walked with him. After appearing to his disciples, Jesus ascended to be seated at the right hand of God.

The right hand of God has always been a position of power. There, his spirit and his power cover the cosmos. Now he is the boss and the lord of everything, "that at the name of Jesus every knee will bow, of those who are in heaven and on earth and under the earth" (Phil. 2:10).

He lives in us, and our life is hidden in him. This means that now we have the ability to do whatever God asks us to do. When we receive Christ into our life, everything that is real in him becomes real in us. That's why Paul said, "**I press on** so that I may lay hold of that for which also I was laid hold of by Christ Jesus" (Phil. 3:12, emphasis added).

Paul lived progressively. When we read his writings, he talks about his own struggles. He said in Romans 7, "I love Christ but the things that I want to do, I can't seem to do. The things that I don't want to do, I continue to do them." You see this guy living in process. There is no straight line in Christianity from immaturity to maturity; there is only process. As Christians, we live progressively. We take on the life of Christ, knowing that he is fully in control of the cosmos and that our abilities do not come from our own resources but from his. In the process of living, we face temptation, our weaknesses, our fears, struggles, problems, and

> ❝ He lives in us, and our life is hidden in him. This means that now we have the ability to do whatever God asks us to do. ❞

hang-ups. But we face them not in the limitations of our resources but in the abilities of the living Christ. Because he is seated at the right hand of God, we can do whatever he asks us to do.

Some of us feel completely defeated because we constantly face temptation. We think, *If anybody ever knew what I struggle with, they would judge me.* I have an encouraging word for everyone who feels this way: Jesus defeated death, and rose again, and is now seated at the right hand of God. We are loved by a king who is in control. Now, live like it!

Paul was saying, "I am going to live like Jesus is in control, like he's seated at the right hand of God. I'm going to press on and move on. I will make only one thing my option—to be passionate about knowing Christ. I press on with total assurance that he is in control."

All of this sounds wonderful, but some still wonder, "What if I'm not good enough? What if I sign on to this whole thing, and I can't do it?" Everything Christ wants from us in this life he has already declared us to possess, in him. Living this type of life is not about being good enough. It's impossible for us to be good enough. If we were good enough, there would have been no need for Jesus to break into human history. If he wants purity from our life, he declares us to be pure. If he wants consistency from our life, he declares us to be consistent. He wants us to be free of the past, so he declares us forgiven. Any demand that he lays on us in the process of following him, he empowers us to do.

> **❝The best thing we can do is to stop trying to perform our way into the presence of God. ❞**

He has ascended to the right hand of God and now dispenses his ability into our life. We're not putting on a show for God to try to get him to love us. We are saying, "Jesus, I can't. But Jesus, with you in me, I can." That is the Christian life.

To every Christian: The best thing we can do is to stop trying to perform our way into the presence of God. Let us instead re-embrace the essentials of the Christian life. Let us once again experience the cross in our own lives, once again experience the resurrection in our lives, and once again draw ability from the fact that Jesus is alive and waiting to come again.

Maybe you are *not* a Christian, and you are wondering, "What am I going to get out of it? What's in it for me?" The greatest thing you can do right now is to drop your guard and say, "Jesus, would you show me that you are real? I don't understand everything, but I get these four essentials. Everything that I can't do, you died for and you can do. When you beat death, you made it possible for me to break the hold of temptation and the things that hold me back. Because you are alive, I have the ability to live."

By receiving his presence into your life, you get a new confidence, a new reason, and a new ability. What greater motivation do you need to come to Christ?

•••

In these first three chapters, we've looked at the *encouragement* and the *energy* of the Christian life. Now, in the final section of this book, we'll move into the *experience* aspect of this life. Life with Christ happens in real time, not in a vacuum, an ivory tower, or an overpriced coffee shop. Healthy progress comes as we make real-life choices about the truth we discover inside Christ's life.

Chapter Four

Do I have to believe all of this at once?

Every year I speak at a series of conferences in Pigeon Forge, Tennessee. I usually do about five high school conferences in a row, so within a few days, I speak to almost forty thousand students. All of these conferences take place a few miles from each other. I speak in one place, get in the car, and drive to the next place, making the same rounds for two or three days in a row. There's not much time between stops, and everything always runs overtime with the skits, dramas, and crazy stuff. I get in the car, speak, get in the car, speak, and so on.

I recall a time when, in between my fourth and fifth speaking spots, I stopped at a convenience store for a soda. At this particular store, I could get the 32-ounce size, or for a mere 25 cents more, I could get the 86-ounce. The 86-ounce is a giant tub that you fill up with a gas-pump nozzle. It comes with two jet skis floating in it—a lot of liquid!

Not thinking ahead, I drank the entire thing while driving to the next school (hey, speaking makes me thirsty). I got up to speak at my last conference for the day, got halfway through the second point, when I realized there were no planned bathroom breaks during the talk. The 86-ouncer was kicking in, and I had to think of ways to compensate. I hadn't brought my speaking catheter, so I cut my talk a little short. I immediately ran down the aisle and shot through the back door. I burst into the bathroom and slammed a stall door behind me.

After I closed the door, I started to hear girls' voices. I thought, *What are* they *doing in the* men's *bathroom?* I heard the sounds of hairspray and some random conversations about Justin Timberlake. I peeked up over the stall and saw ... other stalls. Then I realized the chilling truth: This place was *unbelievably clean!*

That cleanliness, of course, told me the whole sad story of my little mistake. Noticing the stall's door latch was broken, I started to run through my options: *Do I make gross armpit sounds so they'll leave?* I stood up on the edge of the porcelain so the young ladies couldn't see my feet. Clinging to the walls of the stall, I began to do the math on my surreal situation: The door would not lock, I had successfully hidden my feet, but if someone opened the door,

> ❝ I could see it all, from the opening dialogue: 'Hey, aren't you the guy who just preached about the Bible and Jesus?' How would I explain? ❞

I'd be starring in my own movie with subtitles: *Crouching Speaker, Hidden Pervert.*

I could see it all, from the opening dialogue: "Hey, aren't you the guy who just preached about the Bible and Jesus?" How would I explain?

I waited it out, hoping for the best, and soon the girls left. I waited some more, though, until I couldn't hear a sound, before sheepishly stepping out of the bathroom. Great! I had been *totally* unnoticed—except for the entire group of "the popular girls" sitting in front of that bathroom door. They all smiled and clapped for me. I, of course, gave a slight bow and said, "Thank you very much, ladies. I'll be headlining at the next Women of Faith conference."

I was so embarrassed.

The point is, even during our dumb times, and especially during awkward and embarrassing times, whether we know it or not, God is at work within us. We tend to think God only works in us when we've prepared for him. Maybe it's on Sunday mornings or on certain nights of the week. Maybe it's at certain "spiritual" moments that we carve out of our day. Yet the Bible says God is *always* at work in us, through every season of our lives. He's at work in us during the major seasons, the minor seasons, the ones filled with pain and anguish, and the ones that are seemingly insignificant.

Reading this book may be the closest you will ever get to something spiritual, and even this is outside of your comfort zone. But who's to say that God hasn't used every circumstance in your life to bring you to this point? On the other hand, if you've been a believer for a long time, you need to remember that God is continually at work in you, even in the crummiest situations.

God is at work somewhere in everyone's life.

I titled this chapter with a question: Do I have to believe all of this at once? The answer is "No!" That's because God meets us wherever we are in life, with whatever we have and don't have. And he meets us in whatever condition our life happens to be. Christianity is not for just a certain type of person or for a specific demographic. God goes to work on all of us.

In the previous chapter, we learned that when God applies Christ's righteousness to our life, it is a one-time event. This brings us complete acceptance with God and the forgiveness of all our screwups—past, present, and future.

> God is at work somewhere in everyone's life.

But then God calls us to live like the new creatures we really are. This transformation of our lives is an *ongoing process* produced by the life of Christ working in us. This process will continue until we finally see Jesus face to face.

Why are these distinctions important? If we are not careful, it's easy to think, "If I can't live it exactly right the first time, then I don't get another chance." This thinking comes from a nonbiblical teaching that Christianity is either "fully on" or "fully off." But how can spiritual growth be off or on? It's a process.

Most of us have sat through messages in which someone told us we're either *hot* for God or we're *cold*. They told us that if we were lukewarm, then God will spew us out of his mouth. Apart from the fact that the verse being misquoted refers to a church and not to an individual, that thinking is just not true. But because of this idea, many of us have grown up believing that if we aren't fully *on* for God, we should just *click off* and go the other way! Scripture teaches no such thing.

Can anyone be a Christian? Yes! And how do we know this? Because God takes one of the most unlikely people in the New Testament, a guy named Peter, and over time, turns him into someone whose faith serves as the foundation of the church. Peter came from a working family, had some real personality quirks, and made big mistakes in his relationship with Christ. Yet when we see the biblical picture of his life, it is something we admire.

The steps God takes Peter through are the very same steps he takes us through. In this chapter, I want to highlight the stages of the Christian life, the growth process of maturity. But at the outset, I want to make it clear that, after being introduced to Jesus and accepting him, Christian maturity is not a single event. God is constantly at work in us, making us more and more like his Son.

We are introduced to his presence

Jesus stood beside a lake, speaking to a large crowd. The crowd pressed so close to him that he was right at the water's edge. He turned to Peter and asked to borrow his boat.

Now it happened that while the crowd was pressing around Him and listening to the word of God, He was standing by the lake of Gennesaret; and He saw two boats lying at the edge of the lake; but the fishermen had gotten out of them and were washing their nets. And He got into one of the boats, which was Simon's, and asked him to put out a little way from the land.

—Luke 5:1–3

On the surface, there doesn't seem to be much going on here. But the reason Peter was willing to loan Jesus his boat was because Peter *knew* Jesus. This wasn't the first time they'd met. Jesus had been to Peter's house, meeting Peter's wife and mother-in-law. He had eaten dinner with them. In fact, Jesus and Peter had known each other for six months by this time. I'm stressing this prior relationship because, when we read stories like this one, we might get the wrong idea about the Lord's invitation. It's easy to think that Jesus walked along the shore, asked to borrow the boat, and then told a guy named Peter, "follow me"—and for some strange reason, Peter does just that.

It looks like it all happened in a couple of minutes, and that Peter went suddenly from fully off to fully on. No, it happened in the context of their ongoing relationship.

Think of it this way: Christ introduces himself to us in three ways—

As a friend. Jesus borrowed Peter's boat because he had an established friendship with him. He didn't pick some random guy and convince him to loan him a boat. God even uses books like this one to introduce Christ as a friend to those who are in this first stage.

As someone who's interested He's intrigued and wants to be involved in our lives: "When He had finished speaking, He said to Simon, 'Put out into the deep water and let down your nets for a catch'" (Luke 5:4). Only someone who cared about Peter's needs would say something like this. Jesus knew that Peter worked hard to

> "Some readers are experiencing things right now that have been engineered to introduce them to Christ."

make a living and that he hadn't caught anything the night before. Because Jesus was his friend and involved in his life, he spoke to Peter at the point of his need. That's how it happens with us, too. Some readers are experiencing things right now that have been engineered to introduce them to Christ.

As a provider "When they had done this, they enclosed a great quantity of fish, and their nets began to break" (Luke 5:6). Peter was smart enough to know that Jesus knew something he didn't know. Jesus went beyond *knowing* Peter's needs; he knew how to *provide* for them. Jesus never expected Peter to follow him with blind faith. Instead, he called Peter

> ❝ Nowhere in Scripture does it ever say, 'You are just going to have to trust me, that I am who I say I am.'❞

to follow as a result of the things he had seen in Jesus.

No one is ever asked to follow Jesus in a blind leap of faith. Nowhere in Scripture does it ever say, "You are just going to have to trust me, that I am who I say I am." Instead, Jesus always presents the evidence and then introduces himself as the one who can be trusted.

Jesus did the same thing with Zaccheus. He introduced himself and then invited himself to have lunch at Zaccheus' house—just so he could spend time with the man. God never requires that we follow him in irrationality. Instead, we step into a process where we are introduced to his presence through his work and through relationships with other believers and Bible studies.

Some reading this book are at this stage in the process. You are at a point of willingness to be introduced to Jesus. You are touching the things of God for the very first time, seeing him in a different way than you ever have before. Other readers have been around religion their entire lives, but this understanding of the process is fresh and inviting to you. In this process, Christ introduces himself to you and invites you to see him just as he is.

We experience incremental progress

The record of Peter's life stretches throughout the Gospels, but in Luke 5 we read a story compressed in time. Here we see the incremental stages this man goes through in his discovery of Christ. It's our story, too. As we engage in knowing Christ, we'll experience incremental progress. We will gain some ground in spiritual maturing, then we will lapse, losing some of what we had gained. Then will come another incremental step, gaining a little more ground. We're on an upward trail—two steps forward, sometimes a step back. Here are the stages of the incremental progress:

We start out as listeners "He got into one of the boats, which was Simon's, and asked him to put out a little way from the land. And He sat down and began teaching the people from the boat" (Luke 5:3). Peter was in the crowd listening to Jesus' teaching. He probably thought, *Jesus has been to my house, and I know that he is interested in me.* But Peter had not yet faced the big decision to follow Jesus. He was just listening along with the rest of the people.

Are you a listener at the moment? Reading things like this book to see how it rings inside your soul? The process is incremental. We all begin as listeners. We listen to the truth, we listen to people's stories, and we listen to the worship. We listen with our heads and with our hearts.

We then become learners "When He had finished speaking, He said to Simon, 'Put out into the deep water and let down your nets for a catch.' Simon answered and said,

'Master, we worked hard all night and caught nothing, but I will do as You say and let down the nets'" (Luke 5:4–5). I imagine Peter thinking, "I don't get it, Jesus! We are the professional fishermen, and we fished all night without catching a thing. Why would you ask me to lower my nets now, when it's not even the best time of day to be fishing?" Jesus' request seemed a little bit suspect, but Peter nodded, "I'll do as you say," and he lowered his nets.

> 66 … Someone learning to apply truth to his life, regardless of his circumstances. … No longer just spectators and listeners; now God's truth leaps off the page and into our lives. 99

Do you know what this is? It's an example of someone learning to apply truth to his life, regardless of his circumstances. When we enter this stage of growth, the truth of Christ begins to pervade all that we do. We are no longer just spectators and listeners; now God's truth leaps off the page and into our lives.

Peter isn't yet ready to follow Jesus, but he is willing to let down the nets. His trust goes at least that far. Maybe you don't know how the whole "Christian thing" works, but you begin to try out some of the principles you've heard, just to see whether they work. This is exactly where Peter was.

He had just dropped his nets, and that was all. It was a doable commitment, something Peter could easily enough agree to. "I can do that. I can take what you're saying and apply it to this one area of my life—the fishing area."

We (potentially) become leaders Peter and his crew caught a great quantity of fish, so many that the nets began to break. He called for his other boat to come and help bring the catch to shore. When they landed, Peter came to Jesus and fell at his feet. "Don't fear," Jesus said. "From now on you will be catching men."

I can only imagine what went through Peter's mind. Please remember that there were no Christian bookstores by the lake selling little plastic fish and gospel tracts. There was no theological context for Peter to understand what Jesus meant by "catching men." But Peter had made his decision; he would follow Jesus. "When they had brought their boats to land, they left everything and followed Him" (Luke 5:11).

In the first stage, *listener*, we listen and ask questions, and we are introduced to Jesus' presence. As a *learner*, we begin to open our lives to the truth and allow it to begin shaping us. As a *leader*, we take the truth in, and it begins to saturate our life. Then, over time, we begin to give it away.

Everyone we know exists somewhere in this three-stage process. We all start at different places, with different understandings of the Bible and God. As a result, we may be around people who are doing things that rub us the wrong way.

I can't tell you how many people I've met who beat

> 66 'I got wasted with that guy just the other night. What's *he* doing here? Last weekend I was out partying with him and now here he is worshiping!' 99

themselves up because they don't feel as if they have progressed far enough in their faith. They feel guilty and condemned. They think the process isn't happening quickly enough, that they should be further along and know more, that somehow they are responsible for their own lack of growth. They feel guilty about fighting the same battles, over and over. Instead of staying engaged in the incremental process and moving forward, they beat themselves up. Sadly, this self-induced punishment is all too often redirected toward others who seem to fall below the standards.

Not long ago, after I had finished speaking in Oklahoma City, a man came up to me angry and red-faced. He said, "I saw someone on the third row, and he was worshiping."

I didn't know what to think about the comment, so I asked him, "And that set you off?"

"The problem is, I drink with that guy on Saturday nights," he said. "I got wasted with that guy just the other night. What's *he* doing here? Last weekend, I was out partying with him and now here he is worshiping!"

I tried to be gentle, but I just had to ask, "Well, who do

you think is supposed to come to a city-wide Bible study? Only the perfect people? Only the religious people?

"If we only let the people in who truly understood what the Christian life is all about, then every Bible study room would be empty. We are all screw-ups. In some way or another, we are all hypocrites. We all say one thing and do another somewhere in our life."

This is not a Sin-and-Get-Away-with-It-Free card. This is not a pass to say that you can't help but be a screw-up so you might as well indulge yourself. This is not permission to continue to sin and be careless with life—

> *What shall we say then? Are we to continue in sin so that grace may increase? May it never be! How shall we who died to sin still live in it?*
>
> —Romans 6:1–2

Instead, God meets us with his eternally obsessive patience and extravagant grace. He cuts us major slack in hopes that we'll continue to turn our head, heart, habits, and hangups toward him. His Spirit in us will do the work, if we let him.

> 66 We get a glimpse of Jesus during worship, and at that same moment we get a glimpse of ourselves. 99

God cheers for us that we would press into him with our screwed-up lives and say, "God, I know my life is a mess. I know that I'm bent. But with Your life in me, I know that I don't have to stay that way." Do you see how redemptive this is?

Can anyone be a Christian? Yes!

Can we be screwed up and be a Christian? Yes. But choosing to remain in the process means that we give up our right to stay that way. We're saying, "God, over time, no matter how many years it takes, I'm going to get free of the things that are destroying me so that my life looks more like you." The change is incremental.

We begin an intentional pursuit

> *So also were James and John, sons of Zebedee, who were partners with Simon. And Jesus said to Simon, "Do not fear, from now on you will be catching men." When they had brought their boats to land, they left everything and followed Him.*
>
> —Luke 5:10–11

Peter's decision to follow Jesus required six months of a growing friendship. Jesus invested a lot of hours and days into Peter before he ever came to this point, but once he did, Peter's choices were intentional. Look at what happens in the process: "When Simon Peter saw that, he fell down at Jesus' feet, saying, 'Go away from me Lord, for I am a sinful man'" (Luke 5:8). Jesus doesn't have to say, "Peter, you are a screw-up, you are sinful. Repeat after me, 'I am sinful.' Here, sign a card and don't forget to check this box right here." Instead, when Peter caught a glimpse of Jesus, he saw himself. That's exactly how it works for us. We get a glimpse of Jesus during worship, and at that same moment we get a glimpse of ourselves and where we really are with him.

"Amazement had seized him and all his companions because of the catch of fish which they had taken" (Luke 5:9). In this event, Peter surely realized that Jesus was God. This is the moment of his conversion. He moves from being a *listener* to being a *learner* and then to the natural response of saying, "You are God." His faith becomes intentional, and Peter tells Jesus, "I'm yours. I'm in this thing all the way." Then Jesus asked, "Will you follow me?"

> " Some of us have been believers for a long time, but we've just been flirting with living the intentional life. "

"When they had brought their boats to land, they left everything and followed Him" (Luke 5:11). All of this happened to bring Peter to the point at which his faith became intentional. From this moment on, Peter began to live his life based on his relationship with Christ. Life itself became intentional, focused on the kingdom.

The same will be true for us. Instead of leaving Christ in the book or in a worship room, we begin to take the truth into our daily routines. Our life becomes intentional, something done on purpose. All of a sudden, we begin to respond to Christ's promptings. We sign on to his purpose and plan with our whole life.

Will there still be struggles? Yes.

Will we still fail? Sure.

But the point is, our lives are no longer haphazard.

When it comes to being a Christ-follower, how far are you willing to take it? Will you take it from Sunday morning and then leave it Sunday afternoon? Or are you willing to take intentional living into the rest of your week? How far are you willing to take it?

> It's time for us to live intentionally: 'From this point on, everything I do will be influenced by my relationship with Christ.'

Jesus took it all the way to the cross saying, "I'm willing to go all the way." And even though Peter made some horrible mistakes, he refused to back down from intentional living. His choices ultimately led him to be crucified upside down for the name of Jesus.

Where are you in the process right now? Are you willing to take one step closer, moving from being a listener to a learner, from a learner to a leader? Are you willing to move from being introduced to his presence to engaging in the life?

Others of us who are already insiders may need to pray, "God, help me break out of everything that is not of you: my anger, my guilt, my condemnation, my intolerance toward those who aren't where I am in the process. God, help me to apply your truth in those areas." Some of us have been believers for a long time, but we've just been flirting with living the intentional life. It's time for us to live intentionally: "From this point on, everything I do will be influenced by my relationship with Christ."

Once our movement toward God becomes intentional, he takes us through experiences that spotlight the distance between our true position and where we need to be. These experiences can remove whatever might rob us of progress in Christian growth. And these experiences have a name: failure. That's the focus of our next chapter.

Chapter Five

WHY DOES GOD LET SIFT HAPPEN?

If you've ever attended a Little League baseball game, you know how wild things can get on the field (and in the stands). The next batter up is five-year-old Brandon. The umpire places the ball on the batting tee, and Brandon takes aim, swings, and knocks the ball into the infield. He throws his bat behind him and sprints with all his might to second base. Everyone in the stands can't help but laugh. Everyone, that is, except Brandon's dad.

But suppose the pros played like the kids play? I can just imagine a Yankees vs. Red Sox game with all the Little League flub-ups. Alex Rodriguez drives one down the right-field baseline and runs to the pitcher's mound. The announcer picks up the play by play: "Rightfielder Nixon will have to hustle to keep this one out of the corner, folks. A-Rod runs to … the pitcher's mound; we don't know why. His parents aren't here today, but there's a guy in the stands screaming at Rodriguez about first base. He also appears to be referring to A-Rod's family ancestry in a disparaging manner. Jimmy, what do you think? ..."

At the kids' games, there's always a parent who loses it when little Billy does something wrong. We wouldn't normally think of such an episode as a *spiritual* moment, but it is. This is the moment when sift happens. This is the moment when we hit ourselves squarely in the face with the frying pan of *who we really are.* It's not pretty, but it's not supposed to be. It's sift, and it happens.

We'll experience plenty of such times. God has designed these situations to sift us out. I want to demonstrate this situation of sifting so it will be easier to spot in our lives. When we're able to recognize sifting for what it is, we won't mistake it as some random act of evil crashing into our days.

God sets up times of sifting, not to harm us, not to hurt us, but to do us good. A great biblical example occurs just before Jesus' crucifixion. He was talking to his disciple Peter. Everything we need to know about sifting comes out of these four verses:

> *"Simon, Simon, behold, Satan has demanded permission to sift you like wheat; but I have prayed for you, that your faith may not fail; and you, when once you have turned again, strengthen your brothers."*
>
> *But he said to Him, "Lord, with You I am ready to go both to prison and to death!"*

And He said, "I say to you, Peter, the rooster will not crow today until you have denied three times that you know Me."

—Luke 22:31–34

Can you see Jesus preparing Peter for the sifting he would soon face? It would happen in a brief moment. It wouldn't be a season of time, but a situation. It certainly wouldn't take weeks or months. In the life committed to Christ, such situations are designed to sift us, to separate the good from the bad, separating what is of the Lord and what is not of the Lord.

Why does God let sift happen? Five facts describe the process. Knowing these facts will help us spot sifting when it's happening to us.

Predicted to provoke

"I say to you, Peter, the rooster will not crow today until you have denied three times that you know Me."

—Luke 22:34

When Jesus made this statement to Peter, he wasn't indulging in a wild guess: "I *think* you're going to deny me, and I'm pretty sure it's going to happen around six o'clock." No, Jesus knew

> In the life committed to Christ, such situations are designed to sift us, to separate the good from the bad.

Peter would deny him, and he knew when it would happen. God knows our sifting situations coming, and he will even give us the head's up that they're approaching. In addition, we can *expect* other predictable outcomes to go along with sifting:

- *You will be sifted.* Sifting is a normal part of our life in Christ. It is unavoidable, and everyone experiences it.
- *You will be targeted in the area of your confidence, during crisis.* This is the place we might least expect sifting. But this is exactly where it's most likely to happen.
- *You will fail.* Everyone does. That's neither good news nor bad news; it's just the news. This failure is for our good, designed so that we'll "fail forward."
- *You will be shocked by your own behavior.* Sifting surfaces the worst about us. We'll think, "I never thought I would do that. I never saw that coming. I'm usually not like that." We will be shocked, but God won't be. Remember, he predicted it, so he knew it would happen.
- *You will be better for it—and more useful for the kingdom in the future.* Sifting is not an enjoyable experience. But the difference it makes benefits both you and God's kingdom.

"Sift happens" is not just a possibility; it's a prediction. I think this phrase would make a great T-shirt to sell at Christian conferences all across America. It's the story of our lives with Christ. The situation of sifting separates out what is from him and what is not from him. It brings these differences clearly to our attention.

Permitted for purpose

Sifting isn't the same as suffering. Suffering is primarily *external* (recall Old Testament Job: He lost his family, his possessions, his wealth, and his health). Sifting is principally *internal*, aimed at producing brokenness within our hearts toward the character and will of God. God does not use suffering to accomplish his purposes in us. Suffering has deconstructive potential; sifting is always constructive.

God not only *predicts* that sifting will take place, but he *allows* the situation to happen. "Simon, Simon, behold, Satan has demanded permission to sift you like wheat." (Luke 22:31). The phrase "demanded permission" means that Satan had indeed obtained permission from God to sift Peter. So God permitted the sifting ... but *why?* Here's what I suggest:

To transform our natural responses The moment we gave our lives to Christ, we entered into a relationship with God that initiated a life-long process of becoming like Jesus Christ. This is God's number one agenda for every believer. Throughout our lives, God will bring us through situations of sifting in our relationships, in our jobs, in our finances, and in our faith-walk with him. The goal is to get us to look like

> **The goal is to get us to look like Jesus in our natural responses.**

Jesus in our natural responses. He allows the sifting because of our relationship with him.

Many people have built their faith entirely on sentimentality and emotion. It is warm and fuzzy but has no depth to weather life's storms. When things are good, their faith glows; when things get bad, their faith … goes. God sifts us all to remove the sentiment and to develop within us a robust faith for real life.

To help us confront our true selves The truth about most of us, including myself, is that we have over-inflated opinions of ourselves. Many of us think we have a firm grip on faith. God often puts such people in situations that force them to look at themselves for what they truly are.

Peter was so in love with Jesus that he never dreamed he'd deny ever knowing him! In the upper room, when Jesus and his disciples gathered for their last meal together, Peter declared a readiness to do anything for Jesus, even die for him.

Such an outburst was typical of impetuous Peter. He was the first to speak before thinking, the first to jump out of the boat and swim to meet Jesus on the shore. Peter would draw his sword and cut off the ear of a soldier coming to arrest Jesus. Then, when it would be quite dangerous to be known as a Jesus-follower, Peter said, "I never knew the guy!" Jesus allowed this man to be sifted so he could see himself in the truest light.

God doesn't allow the sifting to harm us. But he does allow us to see who we really are without Christ—and who we are with him.

To bring lasting change Sifting is a tool for change that God permits. He lets events shake us up and allows us to fail at the point of our greatest confidence. The very thing we said we would never do will be the thing we choose to do in the sifting situation. When we fail, we despise the way we have behaved. Yet the experience will be quite useful when we face a similar challenge in the future.

To benefit others Our siftings make us better, so we can properly influence the lives of others. We will come out stronger and better able to serve in Christ's kingdom. Without a doubt, God will use the sifting experience to help others as he grows them in the same holiness he is growing in us. He wants all believers to become more like Christ, and he uses these experiences to help bring this to pass.

> " The very thing we said we would never do will be the thing we choose to do in the sifting situation. "

Planned for purity

"Simon, Simon, behold, Satan has demanded permission to sift you like wheat."

—Luke 22:31

Once the wheat is cut and gathered, harvesters strip individual kernels from the heads of the grain, putting them in piles. But the grain isn't yet ready for use; it must now be sifted.

> **What is interesting is that both God and Satan use the same process.**

The farm worker would shovel piles of grain into a sifter, a four-foot square frame with a screened bottom. Another worker would vigorously shake this wooden frame back and forth, causing the dirt and the chaff to fall through the screen onto the ground. The pure kernels of grain remain.

Sifting is quite obviously a purifying process. It separates what is useless from what is valued. The process includes turmoil, stress, and shaking. In the same way, God allows sifting situations to remove the bad from the good of the believer.

What is interesting is that both God and Satan use the same process. But Satan intends events for harm and destruction, to discourage us and weaken our faith. God intends them for our benefit and help, to prove our faith as being strong and growing. God sifts us for good, to place us in a position of greater service. As we rely on his Spirit, we are carried through the tough time into a new place of purity and usefulness.

Peter had said two things to Jesus about himself: "I will never *leave* you" and "I will never *betray* you." Later that same night, when Peter denied Jesus, he failed in his two areas of strength: as a friend and as a disciple. In Matthew 26, we have the most detailed account of Peter's denial. At one of Jesus' trials, Peter stood at the back of the crowd, just so he could watch what was happening.

"You're the one who used to run with Jesus, aren't you?" somebody asked.

"No. You must be thinking of someone else."

Just a few moments later, another person said, "I recognize your accent. I'm sure you're one of his disciples."

This time, Peter cursed before saying, "No, I have never known him, and I don't know who he is."

When a third person made yet another link between him and Jesus, Peter replied, "I'm telling you for the last time, I don't know him."

At that very moment, the rooster crowed, and Jesus passed through the courtyard. He stopped and looked right at Peter. Can you imagine the look on Jesus' face? I'm sure there was grace there, but the look also must have communicated, *Peter, you've always been like that. You are just now seeing yourself for the very first time.*

Matthew reports that Peter wept bitterly. He didn't just sniffle and shed a few tears. This experience broke him, it stripped him. He had been sifted. For the first time in his life

Peter said, "God, I've always been this way. I've had it in me to betray you all along. I'm much weaker than I thought I was." When Peter saw himself as he truly was, it's almost as if God said, "Alright, Peter. Now I can really start to work with you."

Sifting works the same way in our lives. We all have areas of confidence where we have overrated ourselves. There will come a time when God drops us into a situation, and we'll be sifted at that very point. We will do the very thing we swore we would never do.

If we move through the sifting situation correctly, we'll see our true selves. God will have shown us the difference between the bad and the good. But he also sees to it that we have full access to his strength and protection. If in the moment of sifting we cry out for the Lord's help, it's almost as if heaven says, "Alright, now we can work together." Only as we move beyond our overrated "self images" will we ever know God at the deepest level. And only at these times are we ever fully used by him.

How does this look in the most practical terms? Below are three real-life examples. Honestly look for yourself in these situations of sifting.

> " Only as we move beyond our overrated 'self images' will we ever know God at the deepest level. "

In deciding for Christ
Many of us are convinced we are true believers. Our

evidence is: "I grew up in church, I went to FCA, and I was in Young Life. I dated a Christian. I've got a Bible. I've always kind of agreed with the things of God."

If this is you, at some point God will drop you into a situation that will sift you. It will cause you to ask whether you've ever actually given your life to Jesus Christ. You'll scan through your mind and your heart ... and maybe you won't be able to find that time. If you handle the situation correctly, you'll say, "I've just been religious. God, I've just been trying to be moral. I've just been going through the motions. I've never *known* you!" In that moment, God will move in and take up residence inside your heart.

> " We see ourselves as we truly are— not as blithely faithful in all circumstances, but as merely content when things go according to plan. "

In the times of doubt Some of us have the Christian life all lined out. We know the promises of the Bible, we know how to pray in the Spirit, and we know how to "name and claim" the verses that make everything all good. We would never doubt God, of course, because he's done too much for us and we've been walking with him for too long.

Then we face the sifting. A soul-deep dream dies, a

cherished relationship turns sour, a longed-for job goes to somebody else. And we do the very thing we said we'd never do: We doubt God. In this situation, we see ourselves as we truly are—not as blithely faithful in all circumstances, but as merely content when things go according to plan. We are not who we thought we were. Through the sifting, God is lovingly bringing us into reality. There, the potential for joy is awesome.

In relationships Perhaps we get into a great relationship. In it, we want to honor God with everything we do. After a time, we become confident in the boundaries we've established and truly believe everything is perfect. Then, somewhere along the way, God brings this relationship into a time of sifting. The choices people make regarding the sifting can determine whether the relationship lasts or falls apart. We're sometimes left standing there, scratching our heads. *What went wrong?*

Is one of the persons being sifted, finally seeing that they've made the other person their priority—over and above God? They placed their security and dependence on the other person. Whatever the reason, God's honor inside the relationship has become unstable. God began to sift that relationship in order to restore the balance of the honor he deserves.

If we go through the sifting properly, we do what it takes to return our priorities back to God. At this point, it's almost as if God says, "Now I can use you."

Protected by a promise

"I have prayed for you, that your faith may not fail; and you, when once you have turned again, strengthen your brothers."

—Luke 22:32

We can be sure that when we're being sifted, we remain under God's protection. We may suffer attack, but we're not unprotected. Jesus prayed for Peter, and he prays for us during these times. And if there's one person I want praying for me, it's Jesus.

The promise of Scripture is that God will restore us as well. Peter truly failed during his sifting. He denied Jesus three times and cursed just to make his point. He showed no evidence of faith whatsoever.

In Peter's case, just a few days later, he preached one sermon, and three thousand people gave their lives to Christ. Peter would walk through a town, and his shadow would fall over people, and they would be healed. All of this after his big defeat.

Jesus had faith in Peter. He changed his name from Simon to Peter, which means "rock." Jesus told the Rock, "Your demonstration of faith will be the rock, and I'm going to build my church on it." What happens to people who fail at sifting and they admit it? God restores them, makes them greater, promotes them, gives them more responsibility. And they make a greater impact for the kingdom.

Suppose you've been failing in some sifting situations—

and you've failed to admit it. The solution for you today is to get up, turn around, admit, and go back to God. What if you've made God a promise and slipped back? Instead of beating yourself up and feeling like a hypocrite, just say, "God, I thought I could keep my promise, but I broke it. I know now that I can't keep any promises I make to you because I know that I need you for *everything*. I can't do anything without you. Please forgive me. And as best as I know how, I'll follow you with all of my life." If you'll do those things, you'll be okay.

Performed for participation

Here's a new concept of the cross, a different cross from the one Jesus was nailed to. It's not wood, but metal. And not solid metal, but full of holes like a sieve. It's placed in front of the door you leave your house from every day.

We are to measure our daily lives by the cross of Christ. We get ready for the day and walk out the door into the world. Everything about us, everything we are going to do, must first pass through that cross-shaped sieve. It's not easy, but it's something we have to do if we are set on being Jesus' disciples.

The sizes of the holes change. When we weren't very old in the Lord, the holes were fairly large. But as we mature in Christ, the holes become smaller. Larger holes strain out major boulders, the behaviors and actions that are obvious to everyone. We give these things up for good reason. Highway hand gestures are hard to justify, cuss words are hard to deny. And petty theft is still stealing.

Then, as we become more mature, the holes get smaller. They strain out unhealthy attitudes and some of the more subtle actions. When we walk through the cross every day, God strains out the anger, the worry, the guilt, the regret—the attitudes he doesn't want us to carry into the life he has for us.

> **There is no progress until we have confronted the reality of our own weaknesses.**

This is death to sin. It is saying no to self. It is allowing the power of the cross to sift out the unsightly and sift into us its power and abiding presence. God doesn't deal with every single problem every single day. But over the course of time, as we walk through the cross, we come to know ourselves as different than we were before.

There is no way we can sift out these things for ourselves. Only the finished work of Christ can sift us. As he performs the process of sifting on our lives, we simply trust him and choose to leave the things he extracts.

The cross doesn't move; it's there every day. Its purpose remains unchanged. It stands waiting to sift us, exposing and removing the very things that keep us from becoming everything God has planned for us to be.

You see, there is no progress until we have confronted the reality of our own weaknesses. The season of sifting may seem tough, but it can produce awesome soul-transformation. If you'll go through it properly, it'll provide a greater amount of God's power, deepen his presence in your life, and make you of great use in the kingdom. As we'll see in the chapter ahead, this takes place through a process that lasts a lifetime.

WILL I EVER GET BETTER?

I'm in church every Sunday somewhere in America. That can be wonderful, but sometimes it's excruciatingly horrible. Because sometimes the services I attend don't have anything to do with God.

I've been scheduled to speak after more than my share of crazy stories ... uh, excuse me, "special testimonies." It seems the wilder the tale, the more we think it really is from God. And I've heard some pretty amazing stuff ...

- "I sniffed scotch-guard my whole life. Never was able to take a shower. But then I gave my life to Christ and kicked the scotch-guard habit. Now nothing sticks to me but Jesus!" Everybody in the room says, *"Amen!"*
- "I was a power lifter, and one day in the gym I snapped my arms out of socket. Both arms eventually fell off my body, but I prayed, and God grew me brand-new ones. Now I'm weight-lifting for Jesus."

- "I committed a triple-homicide. I was sentenced to life in prison, but then God miraculously changed my fingerprints. I was declared "not guilty," and now I'm out preaching for the Lord."
- "I was a nightclub singer, and Jesus appeared to me in the form of Frank Sinatra. That's how I knew he was real. I recorded a CD with six cheesy songs about Jesus, and now I drive around singing about him."
- "I was an axe murderer. I met Christ, and now I've written a book, *Axe Me about God.*"

The more outlandish the story, the more we think we can sell it. But here's the problem: Stories like these produce frustration in the rest of us "normal people." We begin to question our own spiritual progress. *Well,* if he was able to snap out of a twenty-five-year cocaine addiction over-night, why am I still a chocoholic? *Why is it taking so long for God to change my life? Why do I still struggle with the same old problems?*

Some of us gave our

> **If he was able to snap out of a twenty-five-year cocaine addiction overnight, why am I still a chocoholic? Why is it taking so long for God to change my life? Why do I still struggle with the same old problems?**

lives to Christ years ago and we're still fighting many of the same battles. For others, God-life is new, and you wonder, *When people meet God, do they really just snap out of all the bad consequences and all the craziness of their lives? Why didn't that happen to me?*

A verse in the Book of Hebrews answers this question. Recall that Hebrews was writ-

> **"They had centuries of history demonstrating that suffering was compatible with knowing and growing in God!"**

ten to Jewish believers coming out of a highly structured, daily-sacrifice-based religion. They now believed in the Lamb of God, the once-for-all eternal sacrifice. But they were asking questions like these as they faced persecution:

> "If this is what trusting Jesus is like, then shouldn't we just go back to our old ways?"

> "Why is it taking so long for us to see any real change?"

> "So far it looks like when you give your life to God, then all hell breaks loose. How can this be?"

The author pens his answer: "Remember the former days, when, after being enlightened, you endured a great conflict of sufferings" (Heb. 10:32). They had centuries of history demonstrating that suffering was compatible with knowing and growing in God!

Why is it taking so long for us to be better? To answer, we first need to understand that it takes *time* for the change to happen. And we have to see the big picture in its four parts.

A crisis softens us up

Something comes into our lives—a crisis, some turmoil, or testing—and it begins to soften us up. This is how it had always been with the Hebrews: "But remember the former days ..."

What were the former days? All of their former days were made up of keeping the sacrifices. Every year, these people would have to buy goats, doves, and sheep and take them to the local synagogue where the priest would sacrifice them on their behalf. Every year, a faithful Hebrew had to do the same thing. The blood of the sacrifices covered their sins temporarily, but it did not remove them for eternity.

The sacrifices were so many that blood would flow out from underneath the tabernacle tent into the streets. Can you imagine how tedious this would become? To know that every year, even though they went through the same rituals and sacrifices, it really didn't bring them anything that lasted? It didn't make them any more like God, and it didn't produce any type of spiritual maturity. They were basically going through the motions for a lifetime.

Somewhere along the way, some of the Jews hit a wall and began talking together. I imagine it like this: "You know, this sacrifice thing just isn't working. We are not any better off than we were ten years ago. Sure, we're following the sacrificial laws, doing all of the sacraments, jumping through all the hoops—but nothing seems to be changing."

In our lives, too, there will be a crisis of some kind. We will hit a wall in which we begin to open up. God uses these moments to get us to wake up and to look up to him. We are softened up so God can teach us two important truths:

What you are facing is too big for you Some crises of life are manageable, but some are completely unmanageable. The more unmanageable the crisis, the more it will soften us up to open our lives to God. The idea is not to wait for the unmanageable crisis, but to heed the warning of the smaller crisis and look to God for his provision.

You need God to handle it Let's say you fell in love with someone, you gave your heart away to them, and began thinking what marriage would be like. Before long, you had your whole life planned out, and then he/she says, "It's over."

You think: *How will I ever get through sixth grade?* God uses these "Come to Jesus" moments to bring us to a point where we say, "This is not working; I need Jesus."

The crisis could be in your job, paying your bills every month, caring for a sick child, or keeping your sanity while trying to balance family, work, and time for yourself. Any of these can be come-to-Jesus moments.

Those moments will be uniquely geared to who we are. I spoke at a single's conference in Houston recently. Afterward, I was talking with a guy and asked him, "How did you come to give your life to Christ?"

"I gave my life to Christ in a line-up dressed as a banana."

That's all he said, as if I would know exactly what he meant. I blinked twice and said, "Bro, you're going to have to give me more of the story than that."

"Well, I got a part-time job at a grocery store where I had to dress as a banana and hand out fruit samples," he said. "After my shift was over, as I was on my way out, I stole a couple of candy bars. They busted me, took me to the police station, and put me in a line-up dressed as the banana. That's when it began to dawn on me that I needed Jesus."

God used a banana-suit crisis to soften him up. What will he use with you? One thing is sure: It will normally hit at the point of your dependence. Several months ago, a guy told me he'd been coming to my Bible study for half a year. I asked him what brought him. He told me he was making a ton of money in his business, but in the midst of that success, he had lost his marriage. "I didn't see it coming," he said. "But suddenly, everything between us just died." His whole world was just blown open. "In the middle of that, I thought I needed to find Jesus."

Our heart is softened, our guard drops, and we realize it's all too big for us. We need God to handle it. This is how we all start the Christian life. Something snaps us into the reality of our neediness.

A conversion of the Spirit

In those sacrifices there is a reminder of sins year by year. For it is impossible for the blood of bulls and goats

to take away sins. … Every priest stands daily minister-
ing and offering time after time the same sacrifices,
which can never take away sins.

—Hebrews 10:3–4, 11

Many of the Jews realized that *temporary* sacrifices weren't providing what they really needed, and they wondered what they were going to do about it. The writer of Hebrews responded by saying that Jesus could be their *eternal* sacrifice. Because he was our ultimate High Priest, he stepped into this world and became the ultimate sacrifice.

Animals never could take away sins, because they could not willfully consent. But Jesus willfully broke into human history and willingly took on the sins of the world. When these Jews heard this, their lives opened up, and they received Jesus as their perfect sacrifice, as the Savior of their lives.

> " We never receive Christ's life by solving our crisis or by doing things that make all of our problems go away. "

At some point, we are converted, and our spirits connect to the life of Christ. We realize that he is the only one who can give life. The irony is that we never receive Christ's life by solving our crisis or by doing things that make all of our problems go away. We receive the life of Christ only when we take our crisis—along with our dependence and weakness—and say, "Lord Jesus, I can't do it without you. I drop my guard, open my life, and invite your Spirit to step into my spirit." At the moment our spirits are converted, three things happen:

Total cleansing We receive total forgiveness. Everything we've ever done, or ever will do, against anyone else, God, and ourselves, is totally wiped off the slate. We're washed clean! (See Titus 3:5–6.)

New community We move from the darkness into the light. We leave the family of the enemy and enter the family of God. We receive a new status, in which all the guilt and condemnation of our old life is cancelled. (See Ephesians 1:5.)

Absolute courage We get the freedom to be who God created us to be. We are no longer under the constraints of the world system, no longer under the law, trying to pay our own sin debt. There's a new freedom to live out the complete life God created for us to live. (See Philippians 2:13.)

These three things happen within us. Our thoughts, appetites, instincts, and desires may remain the same at this point. But there was a conversion of the spirit ... and then suffering. "Remember the former days, when, after being enlightened, you endured a great conflict of sufferings" (Heb. 10:32).

There is a counterattack on our security

The moment we connect with Christ, the enemy moves in to attack our decision. The Hebrew believers who gave their lives to Christ underwent tremendous persecution "partly by being made a public spectacle through reproaches and tribulations, and partly by becoming sharers with those who were so treated. For you showed sympathy to the prisoners and accepted joyfully the seizure of your property, knowing that you have for yourselves a better possession and a lasting one" (Heb. 10:33–34).

> 66 We don't come under attack so God can teach us a lesson. We come under attack because of what we already know. 99

Many of these believers lost their families and their homes. They were persecuted and tormented. Why? Because they decided to follow Christ as their leader. We don't come under attack so God can teach us a lesson. We come under attack because of what we already know. The minute we open our life to the life of Christ, the enemy moves in with a counterattack on our security. He challenges our position in Christ.

A better title for this chapter might have been, "Cheer Up, Bad Things Are Going to Happen." We pray a prayer, and for a time we feel different. Our spirit opens up, and we begin to see the parts of our life that don't match our decision. We still have our old impulses. We still struggle with old habits, attitudes, and appetites that are out of control. So we look at our life and think: *Maybe, when I prayed that prayer, it wasn't real.*

We begin to realize that even when we've given our life to Christ, we still fail and struggle and face turmoil. It's easy to look at all of this and wonder: *Did I do it right? Did I tick God off, so he fired me?*

Thus our position in Christ takes enemy hits. Of course we haven't lost our salvation; we become believers based on the fact that God keeps his promises. But the enemy tries to make us think otherwise.

> **" Growth starts after we begin to believe who we are in Christ. "**

Some of us have spent years under this counterattack, making little progress in Christian maturity. Growth starts after we begin to believe who we are in Christ. Until we understand this, we will continue to give in to impulses, appetites, and urges. We'll keep going back to the same old problems. It's not that God isn't real; it's just that the counterattack is also real. The enemy has psyched us into believing we're not really who God says we are.

What Christ did for us, though, settled the issue once and for all. "He, having offered one sacrifice for sins for all time, sat down at the right hand of GOD " (Heb. 10:12). Just before this verse, the author of Hebrews said that every priest "stands daily ministering." They *stood* because their job was never done!

In contrast, Jesus came and paid one time for the sins of the world, and then sat down at the right hand of God. He *sat down* because the job was finished. Once we sign on to this, nothing can ever take our position in Christ away from us. He takes away our sins for all times. He promises that he will put his laws in our hearts, on our minds, and write our names on the palms of his hands. He promises not to remember our sins anymore. Our position in Christ is secure.

Before I started traveling on my own, I traveled with a crusade evangelist. I heard his sermons every single day of my life for two years and came to the point where I began to doubt whether I had given my life to Christ. I majored in Theology in college. Two and a half years into ministry, working with crusade guys all over the country, and I would sit in the audience and think: *Maybe I didn't do it. Maybe it didn't take. Maybe I did it with the wrong motives. Maybe I didn't really mean it. Maybe I wasn't sure.*

That whole thing just ripped me apart. What was happening? It was a counterattack leveled against my security in Christ. It didn't let up until I finally started to believe who I was *in Christ*. The only way any of us will ever beat the counterattack is to build our lives on the facts:

We've been totally forgiven.

We've been made sons and daughters of God.

We have nothing else to prove to God.

Jesus has settled it, once and for all. We gave our life to Christ. We have a new family, new forgiveness, and new freedom. Now we're called, out of gratitude for all these gifts, to live like it.

> " I had to decide that I wouldn't let my feelings determine the way I was going to live. "

We have to choose to stick with it

I came to a point where I had to decide that I wouldn't let my feelings determine the way I was going to live. I had to look to the facts, and the facts said that when I gave my life to Christ, my sin was removed and forgiven. I received a brand-new status. The same thing has happened to all believers, and we have to begin to live out of this truth. "Therefore, do not throw away your confidence, which has a great reward. For you have need of endurance, so that when you have done the will of God, you may receive what was promised" (Heb. 10:35–36).

The Scripture is saying, "You're going to need endurance. Making it through the Christian life means not throwing away your confidence in what Christ has done on your behalf. Don't toss it out as though it never happened! Choose to stick with it."

For some of us, it has taken years for change, because we were softened by a crisis but we resisted turning to Christ. Some of us were converted in the Spirit but we never moved past that point. And others of us prayed the prayer, but the counterattacking enemy talked us out of it; therefore, we've continued to live in fear, doubt, and weakness. There is a point that we have to finally stand up and say, "I believe who God says I am, and I am going to choose to stick with this thing and live it out."

These steps of growth can require many years of our lives to accomplish what they are intended to do in us. I've identified the steps so you can see where you are in the process of becoming better. Are you stuck in one of the steps? Have you fallen for the deception? Do you need confidence? Don't focus on the time it's taking to get better; instead, see your progress toward becoming the full and complete person God is leading you to be.

> " Progress in the spiritual life is the advancement of what we already possess in Christ. "

After all, progress in the spiritual life is the advancement of what we already possess in Christ. From God's point of view, our position in Christ is secure, and we are already complete in him. This fact helps us to remain patient while God continues to work his character into us so that his purpose can be integrated into the world.

Chapter Seven

WHAT IS GOD UP TO IN MY LIFE?

Whenever I speak at conferences and churches, I want people to be honest with me. For some reason, people think that when they talk to me they should convey how spiritual they are. Recently I was preparing to speak in Houston, and I asked a guy backstage how he was doing. "I can't wait to finish with my internship behind the curtain so I can get out there and start speaking! You know how it is."

All I could say was, "I don't know what your big hurry is, Bro. All the interns I know really enjoy what they do."

There was nothing genuine in this guy's voice as he made himself out to be a frustrated speaker. "I've got all these sermons bubbling up out of my heart, and people need to hear them. You're probably like me, man. I lay awake at night because I can't get these sermons out of my mind; they just flow out of me. You know how that feels, don't you?"

"No, Bro, I don't know how that feels," I said with a blank stare. "I lay awake at night watching the FOX news channel. It takes me two weeks to get one talk ready."

I couldn't relate, because that's just not how it works. Speakers like me don't walk around in little worship bubbles thinking *Sermons, Sermons, Sermons.* (Even as I write this chapter, I'm listening to the newest Outkast CD and playing short rounds of Grand Theft Auto, all while making smoothies.) That's not real life. Nevertheless, many Christians have been sold the idea that if we once have a significant moment with God, then something creepy will happen to us and we will immediately start doing great things in the kingdom, to public acclaim. That's not how it works; that's not real life.

Some people express the idea like this: "I just want to go deeper with God." I always ask them what that means. Then, by their explanation, I find they don't really know. Does "going deeper" mean putting on a solemn face and carrying a leather-bound journal just to drink an $8.00 cup of coffee and write down our thoughts? Does it mean we listen to somber worship music and light candles? Nothing wrong with these things, of course. But simply doing them doesn't take us "deeper with God."

When we long to go deeper in a different way—but it's not happening—then we may get frustrated. The result? We give up and think we can't experience God the way others surely do. When I strip away the "God-talk" from people's comments, what I really hear is: "I have these desires to really know God, but I'm not seeing anything come out of it." The question then arises, *What is God up to in my life?*

Take heart. There's actually a discernable pattern of God

at work in our lives, and it's laid out in Scripture. God takes us through these steps to make us more like him, to deepen our faith, and to make us usable in his kingdom. This pattern is not random. We see it coming through clearly in the life of Paul.

Remember that Paul began about as far away from Jesus as anyone could be. He had made his livelihood persecuting the church and killing Christians. He even confessed that he was *perfect* in his hatred for believers! Later in his life, though, Paul wrote to the Philippians that believers should follow the example that God had set in him. Even when he was not aware of it, God was working through their relationship to grow Paul—until he became the great apostle. Paul wrote about this process (and I've commented on it):

> *It is a trustworthy statement* (which means that God is actively working in our lives), *deserving full acceptance* (this means it applies to everyone). *...that in me as the foremost, Jesus Christ might demonstrate His perfect patience* (what God is doing is not a speedy process) *as an example* (what God took Paul through is what he will take each of us through) *for those who would believe in Him."*
>
> —1 Timothy 1:15–16

Whether we know it or not, God is up to something in our lives. He wants us to recognize and cooperate with him in this. As we look at the four stages Paul traveled, I encourage you to identify where you are in the journey. Paul writes to young Pastor Timothy, and in his letter he reveals God's pattern of growth.

There is a moment when Christ apprehends us

It is a trustworthy statement, deserving full acceptance, that Christ Jesus came into the world to save sinners, among whom I am foremost of all. .... Yet for this reason I found mercy.

—1 Timothy 1:15–16

God's only Son broke into human history to draw people to himself. There comes a moment for each of us when the completeness of Christ intersects the incompleteness of our lives. It is our moment of being apprehended by him.

Earlier in his life, Paul had witnessed the stoning of Stephen, one of the earliest martyrs of the Christian faith. Paul held the jackets of men who threw the stones at Stephen. Thereafter, he sought to destroy the Christian faith.

On one of his journeys, Paul was headed to Damascus when a blinding light hit him. He dismounted, covered his eyes, and listened to the voice of Jesus coming from that light: "Saul, why do you persecute me?"

Paul asked, "Who are you?"

"I am the Christ, the living one."

At that moment, Christ apprehended the life of Paul. Paul opened his eyes and realized that he'd been blinded by the experience.

The moment we give our life to Christ, God gains a space where he can work inside of us. On the road to Damascus,

Paul met all there was to meet of Jesus; there was no more of Jesus that he could get. From that moment on, Paul entered into a pattern designed for Jesus to get all of him.

The worship song that says, "God, I want more of you," is a little bit lopsided. When we connect with Christ, we get all that he has to give. After receiving Christ, the goal becomes us giving him more of ourselves. I'm sure that when we sing, "God, give me more of you," God leans over and says, "No, I want more of you!"

> " I'm sure that when we sing, 'God, give me more of you,' God leans over and says, 'No, I want more of you!' "

Being apprehended is the same as salvation, and it brings to us a new life, a fresh relationship, and the cleansing of our sins. It takes us out of the darkness and places us into the family of God. From that moment on, we begin becoming who God created us to be.

You may have just come to this point. You are a brand-new believer, recently apprehended by Christ. He has gained a place from which he can now administer his life into the details of your life. This is the beginning point of the work of God in you. For you, the immediate goal is not to start singing or preaching for God. The goal is that you would say, "God, get all of me that you want." That will involve an adventure of time, energy, suffering, and joy.

There is a season when we are armed with biblical content

Christ Jesus came into the world to save sinners,
among whom I am foremost of all.

—1 Timothy 1:15

Paul had not always believed this about Jesus. He'd been a Pharisee, an extremely devout Jew. Most of the devout religionists of that day had nothing to do with Jesus. In fact, Paul had established himself as the greatest enemy of the church. He killed Christians, burned down their buildings, and ripped apart their families, all in the name of religious devotion.

For Paul to confess that Jesus came into the world to save sinners required that he denounce everything he'd ever believed. After his blinding on the road to Damascus, he went into that city and spent the next three years studying. He had to unlearn legalism while learning grace. As he re-read the Scriptures, he began to see in them everything they had to say about the Messiah, Jesus. Paul was arming himself with content.

Soon after Paul came from Damascus, he went to the temple to preach. But the people didn't receive him because they remembered his previous persecutions. They tried to capture Paul in order to kill him, but one of his friends helped him escape by lowering him in a basket over the city wall.

> 66 Paul allowed his mouth to get ahead of his life. He wasn't ready! 99

116

Paul made his way to Jerusalem. He began to preach in the synagogue, thinking that he was ready for that assignment, but instead of heaven being released, all hell broke loose! Instead of setting the world on fire, he caused chaos and dampened spirits. Only after he left did the church once again continue to grow in peace: So the church "sent him away to Tarsus. So the church ... enjoyed peace" (Acts 9:30–31).

You see, Paul allowed his mouth to get ahead of his life. He wasn't ready! He was still being armed with content. He certainly wasn't ready to disperse it or dispense it to anybody.

When we are in this season of preparation, the only thing "God is up to" is depositing content into us. In this season, we must remain in the truth of God's Word, because *truth is the tool of transformation.* We can't live for God without living the truth. We can't serve God without knowing and doing the truth. The reason some people have a hard time finding a place to serve is because service is not God's plan for them ... yet.

When it comes to remaining in the truth of Scripture, some of the comments I hear blow my mind. I've had people tell me, "I don't read the Old Testament because Jesus did away with that." I actually had someone come up and ask me, "Isn't the New Testament just like the sequel to the Old Testament?"

One guy recently told me the reason he doesn't read the Bible all that much. "You know that the Bible says 'God helps those that help themselves'!"

"Where does the Bible say that?" I asked.

He didn't know, so he started rattling off books of the Bible. "It's in Galatians ... Ephesians ... or is it Lesbians?"

"Oh. You're reading the Queen James Version, aren't you?"

He nodded in agreement.

I've heard people say, "I think that when God is happy with me, he just winks at me from heaven." Another single person told me, "I believe God causes divorce so he can get other people to remarry." These people need some serious biblical truth-content in their lives.

Instead of allowing God to build content into their lives, many people simply pick up random ideas from the people around them. The problem is, this is not content. We cannot live for God unless his truth is in us. We have to know what the Bible says and what it means.

I met a guy in California who liked studying theology, so I asked him what he was reading these days. He named off three or four authors who were in complete disagreement with each other. What I tried to help him understand was that getting content doesn't come from reading random theology books.

So here's a radical idea: At least once in our lives, we need to read through the Bible in a year. Reading plans abound, helping us get a sense of the context. We need to know what 1 and 2 Chronicles is about and what Lamentations and Leviticus have to say. We need to understand the sweep of the Word of God. Without this, how can we really comprehend what's happening in our own lives? We'll tend to believe foolish opinions instead of what the Bible actually says. So stop overcomplicating your faith with so many voices heralding diverse points of view. Simplify faith by opening up your Bible; ask God to show you what's really going on. Read expectantly, and God will speak to you through the pages of the Bible.

Paul went away to Damascus to relearn the Old Testament from Christ's perspective. Before he was released to do battle for the kingdom, he had to wait until he was armed with content. The point of our joining Bible study groups in church is so that we, too, can take up the sword of the Spirit and use it with skill.

There is a season when we apply truth to our circumstances

Among [sinners] I am foremost of all.

—1 Timothy 1:15

Paul always maintained a sense of where he came from. After his friends gave him that basket ride over a city wall, he went back to his hometown of Tarsus. There he spent fourteen years completing the next stage of development.

This was the season of Paul's life when he began to apply all he'd learned. He'd gained critical insights into many of his own motivations and character flaws. He'd learned how to think about salvation by faith, how to pray—and how to say the harsh things in ways that would be less likely to get him killed!

Are you at the point where God is asking you to *apply* the things you've learned? Biblical truth does not exist merely for the sterile environment of a church Bible study. God calls us to live it, to apply it to real relationships, real problems, and real needs.

In Tarsus, Paul builds a tent-making business so he can support himself and others on his missionary journeys. He spent these years developing relationships with people and using these relationships to test God's truth. The more he applied the truth to these situations, the sharper his skills became. Paul learned how to "be all things to all people," for example. And he learned what it was going to take to connect the life and message of Christ to people far outside the religious establishment.

He was in the process of learning to love people. He was discovering how to work out conflicts and how to apply the truth of God to real-life situations. As hateful as Paul was in his earlier life, there had to be a season where he learned the proper way to pastor people. Taking this time to learn the important life lessons, later he was able to write the Pastoral Letters of the New Testament.

> ❝ If someone says they want to be deep, it's not about knowledge; it's about application. ❞

In all likelihood, Paul was haunted by the stoning of Stephen and the other acts of persecution he'd perpetrated.

His ministry was to include several extended missionary trips, and in many cases, he was going to return to the churches he'd harassed with such vehemence. Now he would stand in front of the very people he had tormented and preach to them. It couldn't have been an easy assignment!

Many believers are in this stage. God is not necessarily asking you to sacrifice your life or to do something fantastic or heroic. But he is asking you to take the truth that you know and apply it to the circumstances of your life.

Depth is determined by application. If someone says they want to be deep, it's not about knowledge; it's about application. Knowing more is not what makes you deep, but applying what you know is. The reason a lot of people struggle with the circumstances of life is because they know a lot but don't do anything with it. They know a lot of theology, know all the arguments and how to debate Scripture, but it never impacts their lifestyle. As a result, shallow, knowledgeable people fill our churches. If all you have is a list of preconceived notions and pigeonholed views of God, then you're the perfect candidate for burning crosses in front yards.

While Paul was in Tarsus, a church begun by a small group of believers in Antioch quickly grew beyond their ability to administrate. Paul received a call to pastor that church. He served there for one year. While he is there, a famine arises in Jerusalem and Paul receives an offering from the believers in Antioch for the relief of the Jerusalem believers. This is the first Jewish-Gentile offering.

There is a season when we accept a commission for our lives

Demonstrate His perfect patience.

—1 Timothy 1:16

God places a dream in our lives, something we long to do for him. We don't know everything that happened while Paul was in Tarsus, but we do know that he started a business and learned how to apply the gospel to real life. He may have started a few churches in Tarsus and led some fellowship groups in homes around the area. But anything he did in Tarsus was only the beginning of his worldwide ministry to follow.

The mother church was in Jerusalem at that time, a city weathering a famine. The Christians in Jerusalem were extremely poor because they had been ostracized and their businesses boycotted. They didn't have much food or many supplies.

In response to this situation, Paul brought to Jerusalem a special offering he had collected in his Antioch pastorate. He and his friend Barnabas traveled to Jerusalem a second time to deliver the offering. When Paul arrived in Jerusalem, people immediately recognized him. Paul had spent years applying truth to his life and living consistently in it. The elders in the church of Jerusalem could see the changes and knew he presented them with no danger. They saw the call of God on Paul's life and set Paul and Barnabas apart for a special work. From this point on, Paul began his first missionary journey. He traveled the commercial trade routes to start new churches and to preach the gospel to both the Gentiles and the Jews.

In these ten years, he would write most of the New Testament and do his most significant work for the kingdom. It was also during this time that he endured his most significant suffering. Some of the suffering Paul endured was ...

twice whipped with 39 lashes;
shipwrecked;
beaten, stoned, and left for dead;
afflicted with an unremovable "thorn in the flesh."

It took Paul a long time to get to this point of powerful ministry (and worthiness to share in Christ's sufferings). It didn't happen the day after he was blinded on the road to Damascus.

In the New Testament days, when anyone said they wanted to be deep with God, what they meant was they wanted to be a martyr for their faith! When people say to me, "I want to go deeper," I wonder whether they want to be stoned, boiled in oil, or crucified upside down. To the New Testament believer, this is what being deep meant. Paul was a man who waited a great number of years for the privilege of suffering for Christ.

God had to work in Paul's life, and it required time. From the time he met Christ on the road to Damascus to the time he first went to Jerusalem, Paul spent three years rereading the Old Testament, studying it from his new viewpoint of a believer in Christ. After this, he traveled to Jerusalem to preach for fifteen days and discovered that he was not yet ready for that assignment.

He then traveled to Tarsus, where he lived and worked for fourteen years. He then pastored the church in Antioch for one year before returning to Jerusalem, where he was commissioned as an apostle.

> **"When it comes to spiritual growth, there are no shortcuts or spiritual steroids."**

If we add up the days of this timeline, we get eighteen years. Paul spent almost two decades of his life being readied to complete God's purpose for his life. Eighteen years of learning, trying, struggling, applying, failing, standing up and launching out, and reevaluating. It took eighteen years of content and application to make Paul ready.

God is always at work in us, and he is always up to something in our lives. Some of us are at the point where God has commissioned us to begin to do something. The dream you had when you first met God is still alive, and he has been forming you, sanding and shaping you, to be ready for everything that dream will hold.

When we open ourselves up to the full process of the Christian life, we give God the right to deconstruct us and reconstruct us as he sees fit. If we launch out before its time, we will burn out. Or worse, we'll be tempted to click off from

God and his commission. Instead of rushing out in front of God, let's stay committed to the pattern of God.

When it comes to spiritual growth, there are no shortcuts or spiritual steroids. The thing God is doing in our lives takes time. He works everything in his perfect patience. Don't be in a rush ... because he's not.

READERS' GUIDE

For Personal Reflection
or Group Discussion

INTRODUCTION TO
THE READERS' GUIDE

The Questions for Life series gets to the heart of what we believe. Sometimes it feels like we are doomed to repeat our failures forever. *Why Is It Taking Me So Long to Be Better?* is a question that many Christians wonder about as they struggle to live a life that pleases God. As you read through this book, use the discussion points in the following pages to take you to another level. You can study these points on your own or invite a friend or a group of friends to work through the book with you.

Whether you are just checking God out or desiring to take your relationship with him to a deeper level, let yourself be challenged to change the way you live based on the answers you discover to life's most pressing questions.

Chapter 1: Is there any hope for me?

1. What is the hope for you? Talk about it!

2. In your experience, in what ways was Jesus' invitation different from that of today's churches?

3. What do you notice about the kinds of people Jesus extended his invitation to? How does this make you feel?

4. Why was Jesus' meal with Matthew's friends so radical? How does this apply to your life circumstances?

5. In what ways does the invitation to follow Jesus endanger our routines? Can you give a personal example?

6. What drew Matthew's friends to Jesus? What draws you to him?

Chapter 2: How could God love someone like me?

1. When have you felt unlovable before God? How did you deal with this?

2. In what ways have you seen the strategies of the world played out around you?

3. What do you do with the separation from God that sin brings? What helps you the most?

4. What does God do when we place our confidence in Jesus and what he did?

5. What is the difference between modern, postmodern, and Christian faith? What do these differences mean to you, personally?

Chapter 3: What will knowing Christ do for me?

1. In what ways has our consumer mentality affected how we view our spiritual lives? What examples do you see?

2. What was it that gave Paul his confidence?

3. How does our reason for living shift when we come to Christ? What is your own story with this?

4. According to this chapter, name some of the things God gives us the ability to do. Tell about how you've one or more happening in your own life.

5. What does Jesus declare you to be? How does this impact your self-image? Your sense of hope and faith?

Chapter 4: Do I have to believe all of this at once?

1. In what moments does God work in our lives? When have you seen him most powerfully at work in your own life?

2. Have you felt the frustration of not fully believing everything about your faith at once? What did you do about it?

3. In what ways have you been introduced to the presence of Jesus?

4. Can you identify what stage you are in according to the process laid out in this chapter? Are you a listener, learner, or a leader? Why?

5. How far are you willing to go as a follower of Christ? What is the most likely obstacle or hindrance for you, personally, lurking just over the horizon?

Chapter 5: Why does God let sift happen?

1. Can you identify times in which you've been sifted? What happened as a result?

2. What are some reasons God uses sifting in your life? To what extent have those reasons been fulfilled so far?

3. What is positive about God's use of sifting? How can it drive us toward, or away, from God? What is your experience with this?

4. Specifically, how do you succeed at sifting? How do you fail?

5. If you are being sifted at the moment, how can other group members pray for you?

Chapter 6: Will I ever get better?

1. How has God used crises to soften you up in the past?

2. What does God want us to see in our crisis? Talk about a time when you felt that you were seeing this way—or *weren't.*

3. What three things happen at conversion, and why are they so important? How did you experience these three?

4. What attitude are we to have about the Christian life? But what advice would you give to someone whose attitude "just isn't there"? Suppose it's you?

5. Has a crisis driven you away from God? What choices will you make to return and stick with him?

Chapter 7: What is God up to in my life?

1. How would you describe what God is up to in your life these days? How can you tell?

2. Does God have all of you that he wants?

3. In what ways are you arming yourself with truth? In what ways will you do so in the future?

4. What is God's tool for transformation? How have you experienced it?

5. In what life situations would you like to apply the things you've learned in this chapter?

6. To what extent are you being obedient to the commission that God has given you? Where would you like to be more obedient? What action step have you considered?

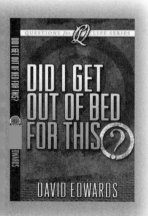

Answers to Life's Tough Issues from the Questions for Life Series

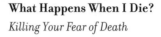

What Happens When I Die?
Killing Your Fear of Death

ISBN: 0-78144-141-2

Why Is It Taking Me So Long to Be Better?
Renovating a Life Like Yours

ISBN: 0-78144-140-4

Why Is This Happening to Me?
Understanding Why You Suffer

ISBN: 0-78144-138-2

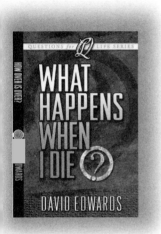

About the Author
David Edwards travels the country full time, speaking to over 200,000 young adults each year in churches and a variety of other settings. As a member of Generation X, he knows firsthand the conflicts, passions, and dreams of this generation.

He has been a featured speaker for citywide weekly Bible study groups in eight states and has authored the Destinations video series as well as his books *One Step Closer* and *Lit*. By addressing the real issues and struggles of today's young adults, Edwards offers direction to generation searching for answers.

The Word at Work Around the World

A vital part of Cook Communications Ministries is our international outreach, Cook Communications Ministries International (CCMI). Your purchase of this book, and of other books and Christian-growth products from Cook, enables CCMI to provide Bibles and Christian literature to people in more than 150 languages in 65 countries.

Cook Communications Ministries is a not-for-profit, self-supporting organization. Revenues from sales of our books, Bible curricula, and other church and home products not only fund our U.S. ministry, but also fund our CCMI ministry around the world. One hundred percent of donations to CCMI go to our international literature programs.

CCMI reaches out internationally in three ways:

· Our premier International Christian Publishing Institute (ICPI) trains leaders from nationally led publishing houses around the world.

· We provide literature for pastors, evangelists, and Christian workers in their national language.

· We reach people at risk—refugees, AIDS victims, street children, and famine victims—with God's Word.

Word Power, God's Power

Faith Kidz, RiverOak, Honor, Life Journey, Victor, NexGen — every time you purchase a book produced by Cook Communications Ministries, you not only meet a vital personal need in your life or in the life of someone you love, but you're also a part of ministering to José in Colombia, Humberto in Chile, Gousa in India, or Lidiane in Brazil. You help make it possible for a pastor in China, a child in Peru, or a mother in West Africa to enjoy a life-changing book. And because you helped, children and adults around the world are learning God's Word and walking in his ways.

Thank you for your partnership in helping to disciple the world. May God bless you with the power of his Word in your life.

For more information about our international ministries, visit www.ccmi.org.

Additional copies of *WHY IS IT TAKING ME SO LONG TO BE BETTER?*
and other NexGen titles are available
from your local bookseller.
Look for the other books in the Questions for Life series:

WHAT HAPPENS WHEN I DIE?
DID I GET OUT OF BED FOR THIS?
HOW SAFE AM I?
HAS GOD GIVEN UP ON ME?
WHY IS THIS HAPPENING TO ME?

If you have enjoyed this book,
or if it has had an impact on your life,
we would like to hear from you.

Please contact us at:

NEXGEN BOOKS
Cook Communications Ministries, Dept. 201
4050 Lee Vance View
Colorado Springs, CO 80918
Or visit our Web site: www.cookministries.com

NE✗GEN®

Building the New Generation of Believers